By-Elections:
Essays of the Nations

JOHN AULT

First Published in the UK in 2015

Institute of Cornish Studies
University of Exeter
Treliever Road
Penryn
Cornwall
TR10 9FE

The moral right of John Ault and others to be identified as the authors of this work has been asserted in accordance with the Copyright, Designs and Patents Act 1988.

Worldwide Distribution and Sales by:
Create Space
Amazon Books
5 Rue Plaetis, L-2338, Luxembourg
www.createspace.com
www.amazon.co.uk

International sales and permissions contact:
Amazon

No part of this publication may be reproduced, stored in a retrieval system, or transmitted, in any form or by any means, electronic, mechanical, photocopying, recording or otherwise without the prior consent of the publisher. A catalogue record for this book is available from the Library of Congress and the British Library.

Copyright © 2015 John Ault et.al.
All rights reserved.
ISBN: 1514773511
ISBN-13: 978-1514773512

To
Steven and Steffan

CONTENTS

	Acknowledgments	i
1	Introduction	9
2	Plymouth Sutton 1919	21
3	Newport 1922	35
4	Kilmarnock 1933	47
5	Carmarthen 1966	61
6	Lincoln 1973	79
7	Fermanagh & South Tyrone 1981	91
8	Mitcham & Morden 1982	119
9	Northern Ireland 1986	133
10	Dunfermline & West Fife 2006	147
11	Bibliography	163
12	INDEX	173

ACKNOWLEDGMENTS

I would like to thank the contributors to this book for their kind permission to publish their work, many of whom are former students at the University of Exeter. I would especially like to thank Willie Rennie, leader of the Scottish Liberal Democrats, who gives a fascinating insight into life as a by-election candidate. Moses Harrison has kindly assisted with copywriting some of the work and Alexandre Ollington has been of great assistance in producing the final printed version which you are now reading.

ABOUT THE AUTHORS

John Ault is an Associate Research Fellow at the University of Exeter where he gained his PhD in 2014. He has been involved in many by-election campaigns himself as a campaigner and agent. He was Liberal Democrat agent for four seats between 1999 and 2002: Eddisbury, Wigan, Preston and Ogmore. His interest in elections has led him to be an OSCE international election observer as well as an Election Commission observer within the UK. He now lectures on British Politics and UK Elections and Referendums at Exeter. He has previously written on inter-war by-elections and their impact on wider UK elections.

Daniel Burrill was born in Cardiff but grew up in Henllys, a village near the town of Cwmbran in South Wales. He applied to read History at the University of Exeter due to having a keen interest in the subject having always done well at secondary school at both GCSE and A-level. His dissertation focussed on the British class structure in post-war London and he subsequently gained a 2:1 degree at the Penryn campus of the university. Since graduating in 2014 he has been working on a graduate programme in London.

Ryan Davies is a graduate from the University of Exeter in History. His academic interests include environmental history and Socialist political history. He wrote his dissertation on the Communist Party of Great Britain during their troublesome year of 1956. Ryan is currently working for the Civil Service in his home town of Newport, South Wales, and in his spare time maintains an active lifestyle with golf and weightlifting, in an attempt to offset his great love for food and cooking.

Miles Fowler is a History Graduate from the University of Exeter (Penryn Campus). He has aspirations of becoming a Teacher and since graduating University in July 2014, has been working as a Teaching Assistant at Handcross Primary School in West Sussex which he enjoys immensely. He is very active in his spare time and enjoys skateboarding, surfing, rock climbing, and reading. Miles has close familial links with Cornwall, and still regularly visits the West Country having enjoyed his time there learning about Cornish History, being the recipient of the Richard Angove prize in 2014.

Ben Manley attended Poole Grammar school from 2005 to 2011 before attending Exeter University Penryn Campus. There, he read History and Politics and graduated with a 2:1 in July 2014.

Ben has a breadth of interests in politics both domestically and globally with his dissertation focussing on events during the Arab Spring in North Africa. He has just graduated from the Royal Military Academy Sandhurst. His interests outside of work include sport, reading and travelling. His younger brother, who attends Warwick University, is also studying History.

Camelia Manzoori is a history graduate originally from Winchester, now living and working in London. She has a particular interest in historical perceptions of identity both locally and nationally in Britain in the early part of the 20th century. Her dissertation was on Antarctic exploration and nationalism. She is hoping to rejoin the Celtic fringe and move back to Cornwall in the near future!

Iain Miller studied History at the University of Exeter, Penryn Campus, and graduated in the summer of 2014. During his time studying he played rugby for the University team, Camborne School of Mines RFC, and was made captain in his final year. Since graduating, Iain has pursued a career in finance, working as a pensions' administrator for small to medium sized company schemes. After just under a year in this job he decided to take some time out and is currently backpacking around the world, taking in New Zealand as well as North and South America. When he returns he hopes to pursue a career in international relations and/or politics.

Willie Rennie was elected as a Member of the Scottish Parliament for Mid-Scotland and Fife in 2011 and shortly afterwards became leader of the Scottish Liberal Democrats. From 2006 to 2010 he was MP for Dunfermline and West Fife which he won in the by-election of February 2006. His chapter is this book is a personal memoire of the events that surrounded his eventual victory. He has previously been Chief Executive of the Scottish Liberal Democrats and then the party's Chief of Staff in the newly created Scottish Parliament. Following the 2010 general election in 2010 he became special adviser to the new Liberal Democrat Secretary of State for Scotland before contesting the Scottish Parliamentary elections in 2011.

Rory Tinman grew up in County Down, Northern Ireland. Although very much a product of post-Troubles Ulster, he is interested in the transgenerational reverberations of the conflict and its memorialisation. Rory works as a freelance broadcast journalist and researcher and has contributed to productions for Channel 4 and the BBC. For his chapter in this book, Rory interviewed Rickard O'Rawe, a prisoner and prison press officer at the time of the by-election, whose account of his time in Long Kesh and the hunger strikes can be read in his book *Blanketmen*. Rory also interviewed Danny Morrison, a press officer on the outside who was heavily involved in the election campaign and who acts as chair of the Bobby Sands Trust.

Tom Wowk is from Chorley in Lancashire and graduated from the University of Exeter, in History and Politics. At Exeter his dissertation evaluated the impact of the Earl's Court rally on the fortunes of Oswald Mosley's British Union of Fascists. Tom is an enthusiastic football coach and now works as an Associate Consultant at Michael Page, working in Manchester for the Procurement and Supply Chain division, specialising in the recruitment of both Purchasing and Supply Chain roles.

JOHN AULT

INTRODUCTION

Parliamentary by-elections are a key part the UK's political landscape. They constitute a brief, but often penetrating, insight into the attitudes of the real electorate between general elections which opinion polls tend only to offer on a more national scale.

By-elections also afford the electorate an unparalleled opportunity to have their say on the government of the day or issues in their local area. This has led the by-election to be something of a minority sport amongst political insiders and can constitute a significant event for a sitting government or Prime Minister. They can be, to paraphrase Tony Benn, 'signposts or weather cocks'. Although Benn used this phrase to describe types of politician it can also be used to describe the impact of a by-election, or series of by-elections, and their impact on political debate.

In this book I have brought together a collection of by-elections which have promoted the cause of a nationalist party, affected its progress or seen nationalism (or regionalism) form a key part of the debate that affected the result.

By-election observers will be unsurprised to see the inclusion of the 1966 Carmarthen by-election which saw the election of Gwynfor Evans, the first MP for Plaid Cymru, but they may be equally surprised to see the exclusion of the first Scottish Nationalist victory at Motherwell in 1945 or the spectacular success of Winnie Ewing at Hamilton in 1967. Of course, by-elections if they are to be signposts or weather cocks need to be understood in the context in which they take place.

It may seem odd to include by-elections in England that might have nationalist influences alongside Scotland, Wales and Northern Ireland. However, their nationalist sentiments can be equally identifiable as the more recent view of separatist nationalism. In this book I have decided to look at seats across the UK from the period beginning just after the First World War.

Scotland

In Scotland two by-elections which are often passed over in the fortunes of the rise of Scottish nationalism are Kilmarnock in 1933 and Dunfermline and West Fife in 2006. I have selected both for different reasons.

Kilmarnock is much overlooked in the rise of the Scottish nationalist movement, as the nationalist cause was unintentionally given a political vacuum to fill, by a contest which saw three Labour parties contesting the seat in 1933. The nationalist candidate, though not at this point an official SNP candidate (the party not being formed until a year later) polled a credible 16% of the poll. The candidate would become the first leader of the SNP - Sir Alexander MacEwen. His comparative success in this by-election acted as a catalyst to the merger of the two wings of movement – the Scottish Party and the National Party of Scotland. The three Labour candidates opposing MacEwen represented a Westminster system that must have seemed perverse to the local electorate, being all Socialists fighting for opposite sides of the House of Commons.

MacEwan's acquisition of the protest vote, as Tom Wowk identifies, was the main reason for his comparative success. This is something that is an essential part of the kind of insurgency that is needed for a party that is trying to break into the political process.

The second contribution, concerning Scotland, is by the leader of the Scottish Liberal Democrats, Willie Rennie MSP. His own Westminster by-election victory, in Dunfermline and West Fife in 2006, saw the Liberal Democrats achieve their highest ever level of representation in Westminster (63 seats) defeating the Labour Party in soon to be Prime Minister, Gordon Brown's, political back yard. Rennie's success appeared to challenge any

Scottish rationale of the time, and certainly since. The Liberal Democrats, when Rennie was elected, had only recently deposed their leader (Charles Kennedy) and were in the process of selecting a replacement. A number of those replacements fell by the way side due to various reasons, leaving the contest between the eventual winner Menzies Campbell, Simon Hughes and Chris Huhne. The contest meant that Rennie had no party leader throughout his election and it was considered to be a particularly low point for the party – and as a consequence his own electoral prospects were considered extremely minimal – as Rennie confirms in his article. This lack of expectation was coupled with the recent election of David Cameron as Conservative leader (this being his first electoral outing as leader) and, more importantly, in this historically Labour, sometimes Communist, constituency the SNP might have been considered to be the natural challengers to the incumbent Labour Party.

With the subsequent success of the Scottish Nationalists in the 2007 Scottish Parliamentary elections, when for the first time it became the largest party in that parliament, this seat might have been considered a key battle for the nationalists and Rennie's success might have been a severe setback for them ahead of those elections. However, this Westminster by-election was apparently still seen as being a contest between the 62 strong Liberal Democrats against an increasingly unpopular Labour government, still led by Tony Blair at that point. Rennie identifies why the party managed to steer its way through this troubled period and win a surprise victory for his party. His impressions of the impact on the Alex Salmond-led SNP are both insightful and fascinating. Little would his party have expected, following his dramatic win in 2006, that within ten years they would have been rejected by all but the most loyal of Scottish constituencies in 2015. This by-election played a significant role in the emergence of the SNP as the major player in anti-Labour politics in Scotland as it formed the zenith of Liberal Democrat support but which was soon to return to Labour in 2010: Scotland actually being more Labour-supporting in 2010 than in 2005 apparently to prevent an incoming English-based Conservative government. The political landscape of Scotland looks very different today compared to this by-election victory for the Liberal Democrats.

Wales

The two Welsh by-elections covered in this book are both significant in the Welsh, as well as UK, context. Spanning over forty years it is difficult to overstate the importance of the 1922 Newport by-election and that in Carmarthen in 1966.

Ryan Davies writes about the pivotal election in Newport which is arguably the most important by-election ever, as the collapse of the Lloyd George Coalition government can be directly attributed to the loss of support for the Liberals, in what was perceived to be Lloyd George's political heartland.

Lloyd George's electoral humiliation, not at the hands of the ever-growing Labour Party (which was to quickly replace the Liberals thereafter in Wales) was to the Conservatives. This Conservative victory, with the Liberals finishing a humiliating third, overturned the planned objective of Austen Chamberlain's Carlton House meeting the next day which instead of indicating that the Conservatives should continue their support for the Coalition would actually embolden the Conservatives and abandon their Liberal coalition partners. The apparent invulnerability of the so-called *Welsh Wizard* had disappeared. It precipitated a general election the following month which saw a drastic reduction in the numbers of Liberal MPs, of whatever brand, and was the moment at which the Labour Party became the second largest party at Westminster for the first time.

If a by-election ever deserved the title 'historic' then Newport in 1922 has to be the leading contender: it immediately ended the incumbent government, ended the premiership of an apparently popular Prime Minister and presaged the dawn of a new era in British politics – the rise of Labour.

In contrast, a by-election that stunned the political establishment of Wales, but did not have quite the same UK significance as Newport was the Carmarthen by-election in 1966. Newport may have seen the end of David Lloyd George's premiership but the by-election in Carmarthen saw the effective end of the Lloyd George dynasty in Welsh politics. With the death of Lady Megan Lloyd George, by then a Labour MP, having abandoned her beloved Liberals in the 1950s as the party sauntered into electoral obscurity, this by-election was also pivotal in Wales.

Although the Welsh nationalist party, Plaid Cymru, had been formed as early as 1925 the party had struggled to gain electoral traction in Wales because of the rise of the working class Labour Party and the continuing attraction of Welsh-speaking followers of Lloyd George. This by-election, as discussed by Miles Fowler, was the moment that Plaid Cymru, in the form of Gwynfor Evans, broke through into Westminster politics, signposting the rise in the 1960s and 1970s of Welsh and Scottish nationalism as being increasingly important factors in those two nations. Fowler explains the importance of Carmarthen as it again indicated that the Liberal tradition in Wales, embodied by figures like Megan Lloyd George (though by then Labour), was a failing part of the Welsh political debate. Plaid Cymru's success in Wales may have been less emphatic than the SNP's in Scotland, more recently, but their representation of Welsh-speaking Wales started to become a reality at this point.

Northern Ireland

Although contained in just two articles the two electoral events discussed from Northern Ireland cover both ends of the spectrum of debate within that part of these islands.

Rory Tinman's fascinating article on the democratic martyrdom of Bobby Sands, apparently at the hands of the Margaret Thatcher government, is both insightful and thought-provoking. Although not written specifically from an Irish Nationalist perspective the article incorporates two original interviews with Republicans involved in the hunger strikes of the early 1980s in the Maze prison. They recall their memories of this important turning point in Republican engagement with the political process in Northern Ireland and the British response.

Sands' candidature for the Fermanagh and South Tyrone by-election in 1981 was highly provocative towards the then Conservative government, challenging the view that Irish Republican prisoners should not be considered to be political prisoners. Sands' candidature also ushered-in a more democratic aspect to Republicanism in the north as it showed that they were willing to contest elections, even, in Sands' case, from a prison cell. His victory cast international light on the state of the ongoing Troubles and his death, only 22 days after his election, being a hunger striker, elevated his status within Republicanism to even higher levels.

His victory also effected the UK government to change the law on who could even stand for Westminster, excluding those imprisoned for over a year for the first time. Tinman's article delves into this troubled period in Ireland and Britain's political entanglement and sheds new light into the mind-set of Republicanism at the time.

Iain Miller, conversely, looks at the Unionist perspective and their organised response to the Anglo-Irish Agreement, signed between the Margaret Thatcher and Garret Fitzgerald governments in 1985. The Agreement, which afforded the Irish Republic some limited say in the internal arrangements of the north, whilst accepting that Northern Ireland would remain within the United Kingdom, was anathema to Unionist politicians of all forms. In an impressive act of political unity all Northern Ireland's Unionist MPs resigned in December 1985 causing fifteen simultaneous by-elections in January 1986.

The incumbent MPs for Foyle and West Belfast (being SDLP and Sinn Fein respectively) did not resign their seats but the objective of the mass resignation was to act as a referendum on the Agreement which the Unionists vehemently opposed. However, viewing this general election in miniature as nothing more than a political stunt the nationalists only contested the seats where they had a prospect of victory and Unionists easily won their seats, with one exception in Newry and Armagh which Seamus Mallon gained for the SDLP. This electoral event was significant in the political life of Northern Ireland as Unionism attempted to slow the process of engagement with the Nationalist minority in the province. It seems peculiar looking back at a process which was to be transformed over the succeeding decade culminating in the Good

Friday Agreement and a further decade which saw Ian Paisley move from a position of deeply held antipathy to Republicans to working at Stormont with Martin McGuinness and Sinn Fein. These by-elections, constituted something of a last roar of Unionism's objections to greater engagement with the Republic and the succeeding decades suggest that the nationalism that Unionists unleashed against the Anglo-Irish Agreement seems somewhat out-of-date. Miller's article debates the reasons for these by-elections and how they affected the political dynamics of Northern Ireland and its relationship with Westminster politics.

England

One of the least debated aspects of the impact of nationalism on by-elections in England is that it is often perceived as being only part of the debate for Scotland, Wales and Northern Ireland. Of course, this is simply not true and the three articles about English by-elections attempt to shed light on this through by-elections which have either clearly been nationalistic or perhaps more esoterically so.

The first, written by Camelia Manzoori, concerns the Plymouth Sutton by-election of 1919 which saw Britain's first woman MP, Nancy Astor, elected. This by-election is, for obvious reasons, perceived as being a massive first step for women in politics and it is rightly remembered for just that reason. However, because of this prevailing, even all-pervasive narrative, Plymouth

Sutton is often dismissed as being simply about that outcome. Manzoori, though accepting the importance of Astor's election as being pivotal to women and the gradual move to universal suffrage, also identifies important aspects of the by-election that can be characterised as being regionalist in nature. Centre-periphery debates and anti-metropolitanism may be modern descriptions for a long-held attitude, but the nature of this by-election, though perceived by the London media as being all about Astor, was much more nuanced and Manzoori draws this out in an interesting reassessment of this traditional Westcountry contest. A contest which saw the career of Isaac Foot, though a loser on this occasion, become increasingly significant and his reputation as a Westcountry champion even more enhanced.

Ben Manley writes about the Mitcham and Morden by-election which might arguably be perceived as being a by-election that saw massive British sentiment as it took place during the 1982 Falklands War. This contest was caused by a defecting Labour MP, who had switched to the SDP seeking a mandate for his decision, saw the Conservatives pull off an amazing gain. This was as the height of the SDP/Liberal Alliance's string of by-election successes and this seat might have been considered a good prospect alongside those it had already won. Angela Rumbold's victory seems to have been a vindication of the Conservative government's policy in the Falkland Islands and there can be little doubt that it happened at a time of increased national sentiment which would also see the Thatcher government returned a year later in the 1983 general election with an increased majority.

Similarly, Daniel Burrill's assessment of the Lincoln by-election, which saw Dick Taverne take on his internal rivals in the Labour Party, over the issue of the UK's membership of the European Economic Community has a nationalist flavour. Taverne's battle with an increasingly left-wing Constituency Labour Party led him to resign his seat causing a by-election in which he intended to campaign as a Democratic Labour candidate.

His campaign was solely about the growing tensions that existed within the Labour Party about whether the UK should be a part of the EEC. This aspect of Britain's future identity is something that should be assessed as part of any debate about whether nationalism can play a part in English by-elections.

The evidence that Burrill brings suggests that although nationalism is perhaps not the right word to describe Labour attitudes towards the EEC the debate that still persists today, with the emergence of a political party entirely focused on the UK's membership of the European Union, is one that has persisted in the UK political consciousness. Of course, the importance of the European Union has become so apparent in recent elections that the emergence of UKIP, and its impacts on UK elections, is still yet to be fully understood.

PLYMOUTH SUTTON: 1919
CAMELIA MANZOORI

As this book suggests the significance of a local by-election on the national level has been the focus of much debate. Whilst it is argued by some that by-election results behave as an 'invaluable political referenda on the action of government', others argue that their results are unreliable and prone to local idiosyncrasies.[1] The Plymouth Sutton by-election of 1919 was significant for British politics in several ways, the most obvious of which was the victory of Lady Astor, the first woman to take up her seat in parliament proving a 'memorable stepping stone in Western social history'.[2] However, a closer analysis of the 1919 by-election reveals a broader significance. The selection of candidates running in the by-election exemplifies the extent of the split within the Liberal Party;

---

[1] A. Mughan, 'On the By-Election Vote of Governments in Britain', *Legislative Studies Quarterly*, 13 (1988) p.31
[2] A. Fort, *Nancy: The Story of Lady Astor*, (New York, 2012) p.162

with local Asquithian Isaac Foot contesting the seat in spite of Lloyd George's public support of the Conservative candidate. The broader significance of the Plymouth Sutton by-election can also be found in depictions of the Labour candidate William Gay in periodicals of the time. There was a great deal of criticism of Gay as a pacifist and an unremarkable orator, a direct contrast to public perceptions of local Methodist champion Isaac Foot, and yet the Labour Party still surpassed the Liberals to come second in the by-election. The fact that this result occurred in the West Country city of Plymouth, reflected a period of crisis for the Liberal Party at a national level, whereby the Liberals were losing support in their own political "backyard". Taken as part of wider by-election patterns between 1918 and 1922, the Plymouth Sutton by-election is notable as a reflection of a wider trend of dissatisfaction with the Liberal Party and the National government. Liberal by-election losses reflected the instability of Lloyd George's "Liberalism". The turbulence was sealed by the carnage of the Great War, forcing open 'the way to a profound alteration in the political status of women'.[3]

The candidates running in the 1919 by-election in Plymouth Sutton reflected the wider disarray of the coalition government. The very fact that Isaac Foot decided to run in the by-election showed a continuing split within the Liberal Party. As part of Lloyd George's Coalition agreement for the 1918 General Election,

---

[3] A. Fort, *Nancy: The Story of Lady Astor*, (New York, 2012) p.xii

only those candidates presented with a 'coupon' could stand for the Coalition government.[4] As an Asquithian, Isaac Foot contested the seat against a candidate with the backing of his own party's Prime Minister. The coalition government was termed a 'two headed donkey' as both the Liberals and the Conservatives pulled the government in different directions, achieving little. The depiction of Lady Astor atop of a two headed donkey in a periodical cartoon demonstrates the significance of the by-election for the liberal coalition.[5] The sketch shows Astor as significant in two lights, not only as a woman, but also as a conservative. As a woman Astor flouted 'parliamentary tradition' whilst not riding the traditional female side saddle. As a conservative Astor is seen carried atop the two headed donkey of the coalition government, indicative of the open support she received from both the Conservative leader and the Liberal Prime Minister. Lady Astor is also actively riding the donkey in a certain direction, the conservative direction. Isaac Foot's decision to contest the Plymouth-Sutton seat, despite the imposing opposition of Lady Astor atop a two-headed donkey, illustrates the dissent within the increasingly divided Liberal Party.

Another interesting feature of the 1919 Plymouth Sutton

---

[4] 'The "coupon" was a device employed by the Coalition leaders to indicate which candidates they wanted elected. It consisted of a letter, signed by Lloyd George and Bonar Law, informing its recipient that he was recognized as the official Coalition candidate in his constituency. Its effect was far-reaching. It not only be-stowed the favor of the Coalition on a particular body of candidates, but...repudiated all other candidates in their constituencies as enemies of the Coalition.' T. Wilson, 'The Coupon and the British General Election of 1918', *The Journal of Modern History, 36, 1* (1964) p.29
[5] *The Star*, 29th November 1919

by-election is that it yielded a significantly increased turnout in comparison with the 1918 results for the same constituency. Turnout increased from 59.6% in the 1918 election for Lord Astor to 72.5% for Lady Astor's 1919 by-election.[6] To an extent this increase can be explained away in that many of the forces had not been repatriated in time for the 1918 election on December 14th, this was obviously still an issue in 1919 when the votes were not counted until two weeks after scheduled because of absentee voters still overseas on post-war duties.[7] Other potential causes for Lady Astor's victory shed light on the significance of the by-election in a wider national context. The first explanation for the 1919 result relies on the theory that by-election voting is dominated by "personal votes" for particular MPs; the second is that by-elections are perceived as referendums on the government's record so far.[8]

The first explanation easily fits to the Plymouth Sutton model. Lady Astor became the first woman to contest a seat in parliament and actually take it up: Historically significant in that suffrage to land-owning women over thirty only occurred one year earlier with the 1918 Representation of the People Act. There had been seventeen women candidates in the December 1918 election, all had failed except Constance Markiewicz, the Sinn Fein candidate who in accordance with party policy declined to take up

---

[6] M. Hilson, *Political Change And the Rise of Labour in Comparative Perspective: Britain And Sweden, 1890-1930* (Lancaster, 2006) p.323
[7] A. Fort, *Nancy: The Story of Lady Astor*, (New York, 2012) p.163
[8] S. Price, and D. Sanders, ' By-Elections, Changing Fortunes, Uncertainty and the Mid-Term Blues', *Public Choice, 95* (1998) p.132

her seat.[9] Entirely different to the militant leaders of The Women's Social and Political Union, who were feared and expected by men, Lady Astor's personal role in bringing women and domestic issues to the forefront of politics, meant that she had accessed the household vote in a way her husband and predecessor, Waldorf Astor, had not.[10] Evidence of this can be seen in Hansard records from December 1919: "Viscountess Astor asked the Food Controller whether the prices fixed by the Government have had the effect of restricting the consumption of milk" and highlights the responsibilities of the "Maternity and Child Welfare Act to provide milk under cost price".[11] The household aspects of her campaign, such as organising women only meetings, allowed women to engage with the candidate in the absence of men, this could go some way to explaining the increased turnout.[12] Even Isaac Foot's wife, despite being diligently Liberal, attended a support meeting for Nancy Astor in Plymouth, suggesting that for many history came before politics in the by-election.[13] Topics Lady Astor raised in Commons debates, drunkenness, imprisonment of pregnant women and pensions for widows of servicemen, had great significance in a wider political context. For the first time in British political history, the woman's voice was being heard.

---

[9] A. Fort, *Nancy: The Story of Lady Astor*, (New York, 2012) p.160
[10] *Ibid.* p.xiv
[11] *Hansard*, HC Deb 28 December 1919, vol 123, cols 250-2
[12] M. Hilson, *Political Change And the Rise of Labour in Comparative Perspective: Britain And Sweden, 1890-1930* (Lancaster, 2006) p.168
[13] M. Foot and A. Highet, *Isaac Foot: A Westcountry Boy - Apostle of England: A Plymouth Boy* (London, 2006) p.133

Lady Astor's notoriety among her constituents is evident in the sheer amount of column inches the contest amassed. National newspapers such as *The Times* remarked on how 'her popularity is undoubted - everyone refers to her as "Nancy Astor"'.[14] An article in the *Saturday Review*, although inclined against Astor on the whole, noted her ability to garner publicity: 'May we hope that the Nancy Witcher stunt will now die down? We fear not'.[15] This notion that Lady Astor's success depended mainly on 'her communication skills-her ability to share rhetorically compelling visions with her voters' and her assumed role as 'serious Pilgrim mother' is supported by the film clips of British Pathé.[16] Clips of polling day scenes in 1919 predominantly feature Lady Astor surrounded by children supporters, affirming the theory that by-election voting is dominated by "personal votes" for particular MPs.[17][18] However, what is in fact more revealing in the wider context is the significant absence of publicity on Lady Astor's opponents. This supports the second explanation for the 1919 result, that by-elections are perceived as referendums on the government's record so far.[19]

---

[14] *The Times*, 3rd November 1919
[15] *Saturday Review of Politics, Literature, Science and Art*, 6th December 1919
[16] G.L. Reid, 'Review article: Plymouth to Parliament: A Rhetorical History of Nancy Astor's 1919 Campaign by Karen J. Musolf', *A Quarterly Journal Concerned with British Studies, 32* (2000) p.163
[17] *Pathé News*, 20th November 1919
[18] S. Price, and D. Sanders, 'By-Elections, Changing Fortunes, Uncertainty and the Mid-Term Blues', *Public Choice, 95* (1998) p.132
[19] S. Price, and D. Sanders, 'By-Elections, Changing Fortunes, Uncertainty and the Mid-Term Blues', *Public Choice, 95* (1998) p.132

By-elections typically exaggerate national swings, these swings can be negative as well as positive.[20] The main significance of Lady Astor's victory in the Plymouth Sutton by-election in 1919 is not her victory, but the failure of the other parties. If voters feel they will be negatively affected by their less preferred party being elected, then they will "over-vote" in order to elect the most effective alternative.[21] This dissatisfaction with the policies of Labour and Liberal candidates at a local and regional level, reflects change at a national level arguably foretelling the 1922 general election victory for the Conservatives. Depictions of Labour Candidate T.W. Gay remark that he is not a 'dominating personality' and local newspaper *The Western Daily Mercury* describes the Labour campaign as 'a dark and gloomy one, unrelieved by any sunshine or laughter'. [22][23] Although perceptions of the Labour candidate are significant at a local level, they shed little light on the wider reception of the Labour Party at this time as much of the opposition to the Labour candidate was based on his particular personality, rather than party policy. Gay's position as an 'anti-war pacifist...alienated many of the stauncher and more patriotic trade unionists', as well as Plymouth's strong naval heritage.[24] This stands in stark contrast to the wartime efforts of Lady Astor, 'one of the first ladies who went through the streets at

---

[20] S. Price, and D. Sanders, 'By-Elections, Changing Fortunes, Uncertainty and the Mid-Term Blues', *Public Choice*, 95 (1998) p.131
[21] *Ibid.* p.143
[22] *The Times*, 3rd November 1919
[23] *Western Daily Mercury*, 11th November 1919
[24] *The Observer*, 2nd November 1919

the request of Mr. Lloyd George when he called for women munitions workers in the critical days of the war'.[25] Although Gay was a dependable candidate, 'liked and trusted by those whom he seeks to represent', the contrast in character between him and Lady Astor 'keen for the struggle' is predominantly behind Labour's loss in the by-election. [26][27] What we should draw our attention to is that, despite this aversion for T.W. Gay as a person on the micro-level, the emerging Labour Party still came in ahead of the Liberals in the by-election results.

Public opinion of the Liberal Party during the by-election holds significance in wider context. Price and Sanders argue that it is a 'stylised fact' of by-elections that governments tend to lose them, in this way perceptions of the Liberal Party in the Plymouth Sutton by-election could be expanded onto a national model. [28] Despite the description of Isaac Foot as a well-liked character, 'Mr Foot sportingly stated to me that he yields to no one in his admiration for the social work done by lady Astor' the Liberal share of the vote in the 1919 by-election was only 14.8%, compared to Labour's 20.6% share. [29][30] Foot was 'highly regarded' and an 'excellent speaker', but it was liberal policies and divisions

---

[25] *The Observer*, 2nd November 1919
[26] *The Times*, 3rd November 1919
[27] *The Observer*, 2nd November 1919
[28] S. Price, and D. Sanders, ' By-Elections, Changing Fortunes, Uncertainty and the Mid-Term Blues', *Public Choice*, 95 (1998) p.131
[29] *The Observer*, 2nd November 1919
[30] M. Hilson, *Political Change And the Rise of Labour in Comparative Perspective: Britain And Sweden, 1890-1930* (Lancaster, 2006) p.323

on a national level rather than him as an individual candidate that led to Liberal defeat in the by-election.[31] Assurances that 'his municipal record is a creditable one'[32] did little to alleviate the general sentiment that as 'An out-and-out Asquithian'[33] his classical liberal policies were not an effective vehicle for change. The electoral map was drawn more closely on class lines than ever before, in this increasingly radical climate, the Liberals as the middle party did not seem the best bet.[34] The local *Western Morning News* describes how 'the faded banner of "Peace, Retrenchment and Reform", even in these financially critical days, is doomed'.[35] The wider significance of the by-election results thus lies in perceptions of the Liberal Party. When contrasted in 1919 to the fresh prospect of Lady Astor as a woman candidate, Foot was seen as 'someone who had already had his day and was out of step with the times', Foot had better success in Bodmin in 1922, with the absence of a Labour candidate to draw away radical support.[36][37] The West Country location of the by-election further compounded the extent of this liberal crisis at the national level.

---

[31] G.L. Reid, 'Review article: Plymouth to Parliament: A Rhetorical History of Nancy Astor's 1919 Campaign by Karen J. Musolf', *A Quarterly Journal Concerned with British Studies, 32* (2000) p.164
[32] *The Observer,* 2nd November 1919
[33] *The Times*, 3rd November 1919
[34] D. Dutton, *A History of the Liberal Party in the Twentieth Century,* (Basingstoke, 2004) p.25
[35] *The Observer,* 2nd November 1919
[36] G.L. Reid, 'Review article: Plymouth to Parliament: A Rhetorical History of Nancy Astor's 1919 Campaign by Karen J. Musolf', *A Quarterly Journal Concerned with British Studies, 32* (2000) p.164
[37] J. Ault., 'The Inter – War Cornish By- Elections: Microcosm of 'Rebellion'?' in P. Payton, (ed.), *Cornish Studies, 20* (Exeter, 2012) p.243

The Observer in 1919 described the Sutton Division of Plymouth as 'a typical West Country town constituency'.[38] The significance of this in the wider context is that the West Country and "Celtic fringe" had traditionally been a bastion of support for the Liberal Party. In effect Plymouth was a decidedly a-typical constituency, there were areas of concentrated deprivation, arguably more so than almost anywhere else in Britain, and 'thus fertile ground for the new liberal ideas'.[39] However, after the First World War, the Liberal Party could no longer hold the support it once could. The Liberals' role in the war made them culpable for the failures to make Britain a 'country fit for heroes' and Plymouth Sutton contained 'a large sprinkling of Service men, as well as a number of old time pensioners, veterans of other wars, by whom Lady Astor is beloved'.[40][41] Moreover, the 1918 Representation of the People Act tripled the number of people allowed to vote in Britain from seven to twenty-one million, completely changing the face of the British electorate.[42] On a national level, Labour was portraying itself as the most effective alternative to the Conservatives, whilst the Liberal Party's 'only idea was to turn the clock back to where it stood at the end of July, 1914 and ignore the totally great lesson of the war'.[43] Periodicals commenting on the by-election feature an abundance of references to Isaac Foot as a

---

[38] *The Observer*, 2nd November 1919
[39] A. Fort, *Nancy: The Story of Lady Astor*, (New York, 2012) p.114
[40] *Saturday Review of Politics, Literature, Science and Art*, 3rd May 1919
[41] *The Observer*, 2nd November 1919
[42] Representation of the People Act 1918, *UK Parliament*
[43] *Western Morning News*, 29th November 1919

"local" candidate, 'local leader of the Asquith Liberals in the town...Wesleyan local preacher, and son of a trader in the town', suggesting that Foot was very much seen as the local champion. In a way that future Liberals would campaign using their pavement politics tactics, Foot's campaign also presented himself as within Plymothian Radical tradition, referencing Plymouth's role in the Civil war and 'famous West countrymen like Pym and Eliot'.[44][45] Yet he failed to win any significant share of the vote, supporting the theory of Price and Sanders that voters care mainly about policies, rather than parties.[46] This Liberal loss in their own political "backyard", gains further significance when contextualised among the wider trend of by-election results from 1919 to 1922. It is from this contextualising of the Plymouth Sutton example that we can see reflections of the Liberal Party's national crisis.

However, it could be argued that the significance of the Plymouth Sutton by-election, and by-elections in general, are overvalued and that we can readily ascribe too much to a local electoral snapshot. This view is supported by the fact that the Plymouth Sutton by-election was very early on in the term, arguably, too early for the results to infer referendum attitudes to Lloyd George's coalition. Dutton claims that as a general rule, 'it is

---

[44] *The Observer,* 2nd November 1919
[45] M. Hilson, *Political Change And the Rise of Labour in Comparative Perspective: Britain And Sweden, 1890-1930* (Lancaster, 2006) p.166
[46] S. Price, and D. Sanders, ' By-Elections, Changing Fortunes, Uncertainty and the Mid-Term Blues', *Public Choice, 95* (1998) p.132

governments which lose elections rather than oppositions which win them', but arguably this also holds true of by-elections. Taylor and Payne's argue that the "mid-term dip" is a 'well-defined characteristic' of UK by-election data, as governments squeeze inflation after the election. [47][48] This would mean that the significance of the Liberal loss in Plymouth Sutton in 1919 perhaps means less in the wider context of British politics than this chapter has so far suggested. What is more it could be argued that the by-election results in 1919 could be 'attributed to idiosyncrasies of the individual contest'.[49] This critique that by-elections are purely a reflection of local peculiarities is supported by the economic turmoil of Plymouth in 1919. By late that year there were six thousand unemployed in the city, exacerbated by dockyard discharges, there was 'major dissatisfaction', which could be articulated through a vote against the coalition.[50] However, although by-elections only offer a geographically defined snapshot, 'they are real votes in a real election' and when taken in conjunction with by-election patterns in other constituencies can construct a fairly accurate view of national opinion.[51] The result of the Plymouth Sutton by-election was part of, and exemplified, a wider

---

[47] D. Dutton, *A History of the Liberal Party in the Twentieth Century*, (York 2004) p.14
[48] Taylor and Pane in S. Price, and D. Sanders, ' By-Elections, Changing Fortunes, Uncertainty and the Mid-Term Blues', *Public Choice*, 95 (1998) p.132
[49] A. Mughan, 'On the By-Election Vote of Governments in Britain', *Legislative Studies Quarterly*, *13* (1988) p.31
[50] M. Hilson, *Political Change And the Rise of Labour in Comparative Perspective: Britain And Sweden, 1890-1930* (Lancaster, 2006) p.170
[51] C. Mason, 'Analysis: Do by-elections mean anything?', *BBC News*

trend of discontent with Liberal policies and a lack of faith in the unity of their party. This becomes evident through the pattern of results from other by-elections between 1918 and 1922. Of the by-elections between 1918 and 1922 that actually resulted in seat changes, only four out of twenty eight contests resulted in a liberal candidate winning the seat.[52] This undermines the notion that by-elections are 'local events relatively untouched by such national forces' and massive swings against the Liberals in the 1920 Dartford and 1922 Newport by-election further demonstrated the wider significance of the Plymouth-Sutton by-election in a national context.[53][54]

The 1919 Plymouth Sutton by-election was significant at both a local, regional and national level. On a national level, Liberal Isaac Foot's contest for the seat, against the support of the leader of his party, embodies Liberal divisions during and after the First World War. Lady Astor's victory in 1919 can be explained by two theories, both of which demonstrate the significance of the Plymouth-Sutton by-election in a wider context. The first explanation is based on the idea that local by-elections are dominated by personal votes for particular candidates, Lady Astor being one of the first woman to contest a seat in parliament, and

---

[52] D. Butler and A. Sloman, *British Political Facts 1900-1979*, fifth edition (US, 1980) p.222
[53] A. Mughan, 'On the By-Election Vote of Governments in Britain', *Legislative Studies Quarterly*, 13 (1988) p.33
[54] D. Butler and A. Sloman, *British Political Facts 1900-1979*, fifth edition (US, 1980) p.223

the first to actually take the seat up. Accordingly the significance of Lady Astor's campaign for women's rights and the emerging household vote cannot be underestimated.

However, what is in fact more revealing in the wider context is the significant absence of publicity on Lady Astor's opponents and that the swing towards the Conservative Lady Astor was as much a swing against the Liberal and Labour candidates. Despite aversions to T.W. Gay as a person on the micro-level, the emerging Labour Party still came in ahead of the Liberals in the Liberals' political "backyard". Thus supporting the second explanation for the result in the 1919 by-election, by-elections as referendums on the government's record so far. The wider significance of the Plymouth Sutton by-election is its exposure of growing disillusionment with the policies and the unity of the Liberal Party at a national as well as a local level. In this way, when taken as part of wider by-election patterns between 1918 and 1922, the 1919 Plymouth Sutton by-election provides an indispensable political ballot on the action of government. The triumph of a female Conservative candidate in a city with a strong Liberal legacy, heralded the transformation of British politics, leaving a permanent imprint on the political life of the nation that was wholly unanticipated.[55]

---

[55] A. Fort, *Nancy: The Story of Lady Astor*, (New York, 2012) p.xii

NEWPORT: 1922
RYAN DAVIES

Despite not being a direct part of the election of a government, by-elections are nonetheless important parts of the British political system. Spanning constituencies across the entire country, they help provide valuable insights into feelings, sentiments and political leanings throughout Britain; indeed, they are barometers of public opinion.[56] No matter the outcome, be it re-affirmation of a political party's stronghold in a particular area, or an upset that sees the incumbent replaced by a new, unexpected contender, the results can be analysed and understood as part of the processes of everyday political life and useful in creating cultural and social histories of an area.

As these elections cover all areas of the country at a local

---

[56] J. Ault., 'The Inter – War Cornish By- Elections: Microcosm of 'Rebellion'?' in P. Payton (ed.), *Cornish Studies, 20* (Exeter, 2012) p.241

level, results can be investigated with reference to the specific locality in which they are held, and the factors within said locality that may or may not have influenced the outcome of the vote. Furthermore, by comparing specific studies of these localities we can not only study attitudes present in them, but also look at how issues are treated in similar or different ways within various areas, and why this may be. This can help place the by-election amongst larger scale developments determined by geography. In addition, larger scale temporal developments can also be considered in by-election results; by understanding the machinations of the public and government before, during and after a by-election, we can begin to further see its significance in a broader scale – either by seeing how the by-election fits into long term trends, or how it is affected by short term issues that are present in the public mind.

Newport's by-election in 1922, wasn't, as is often the case, called for a political or social reason at the time, but instead due to the untimely death of the Liberal coalition member for the area, Lewis Haslam. Following this, a non-coalition, Liberal candidate was put forward to the ensuing contest, which contained two other non-coalition candidates – the Conservative Reginald Clarry and Labour John William Bowen, as well as the aforementioned Liberal candidate, Lyndon William Moore. Neither the Conservative nor the Liberal candidates were backed by their national parties in the coalition government; for all intents and purposes, it was a fair three cornered fight for the seat.[57]

Although the cause for the election itself was unpredicted, the actual contest itself and the candidates put forward were highly political. The Labour candidate was standing with the support of his party due to Labour's inexorable rise to popularity and pervasiveness during the 1920s – indeed, the following year the party's first government was formed (even if it was a minority one). Furthermore, being a working class town in Wales paired with Labour's rise in prominence, and with constituencies around Newport, such as Pontypridd, falling to the Socialist party, the Newport by-election was predicted to be strongly favourable for Labour.

After the death of Haslam, there was discussion of putting a coalition candidate up for the seat.[58] However, this was rejected by the respective Newport Liberal and Conservative associations, instead favouring their own, independent candidates to be put forward the contest. This exposes the increased tensions within the coalition and the representatives of the individual parties that made it up; the devout Liberal, Asquith, called the coalition an evasion, a compromise that was barely politics, and many Conservatives also took this view.[59] Indeed, the Newport Conservative Association argued it was better to lose as Conservatives than win as Liberals, a

---

[57] D. Russell,. 'History Lessons For The Conservatives and Liberal Democrats', *Click on Wales*
[58] *Ibid.*
[59] *The Times*, 10th October 1922

statement which perfectly exemplifies the identity issues that wracked the Liberals, and, growingly, the Conservatives, within the coalition.[60][61] Indeed, simply in terms of who was put forward for the seat, the Newport by-election can be seen as significant in that it mirrored trends that were being exhibited both within the party of government, independent parties, and in constituency political battles across the breadth of the country, as well as throughout the coalition's existence. The result, however, is arguably of much more intrigue and significance.

The independent Conservative candidate won the by-election with 13,515 votes, a majority of 2,090 over the second place Labour candidate.[62] This was a huge upset, as it was an almost settled view within the coalition government that Labour would continue their dominance in the area and build one more step in their rise to prominence by winning the contest. Common interpretations of this event argue that because the coalition Conservatives were so sure of the party's weakness and Labour's dominance, they remained in the coalition so as not to split the anti-Labour vote; but, after this shock victory, the members re-assessed their need for the coalition and called the Carlton Club meeting of October 19th, 1922 to discuss its future. This led to a vote of non-confidence in the coalition, and thus the Conservatives removed themselves from it, ending the government. Thus, the

---

[60] *The Times*, 10th October 1922
[61] C. L. Mowat, *Britain Between the Wars, 1918-1940* (London, 1968) pp.79-142
[62] J. Bryant, 'Newport By-election Sensation', *Paul Flynn MP Blog*

1922 Newport by-election has been dubbed the only by-election to ever directly lead to the fall of a government.[63]

This interpretation fits in well to discourses of the state of the coalition and its collapse, arguing that Newport was a culmination of pressures and doubts within the coalition, delivering the killer blow to the government and the Conservative support for it. Indeed, the issues within the coalition have been documented and widespread throughout the primary and secondary literature.

There was growing disharmony within the coalition over Lloyd George's leadership – dubbed the end of cabinet led government, and the rise of the prime ministerial government, many had issues over the premier's 'dictatorial' control over government policy, often overriding the wishes of many cabinet ministers.[64] Thus, the Conservative members of the coalition (except, among a few, Austen Chamberlain) were already harbouring thoughts of discontent towards the coalition due to its overbearing leadership. In addition to this, the Chanak Crisis was a significant issue at the time, with Lloyd George's faults being brought to bear; he had lost his diplomatic edge with France and Italy, Bonar Law openly criticized the action taken in a letter to *The Times*, and public opinion was levelled against the Prime

---

[63] J. Ault., 'The Inter – War Cornish By- Elections: Microcosm of 'Rebellion'?' in P. Payton,(ed.), *Cornish Studies, 20* (Exeter, 2012) p.245
[64] R. Self, 'Fighting One's Own Friends is Hateful Work: Coalition troubles, January – October 1922' in R. Self (ed.) *The Austen Chamberlain Diary Letters. The Correspondence of Sir Austen Chamberlain with his Sisters Hilda and Ida, 1916-1937* (Camden, 1995) Fifth Series, Vol. 5, p.197

Minister's foreign policy on this issue.[65] Thus, the event had the impact of further undermining Lloyd George's authority both in the public sphere and within the party; and, due to outcry such as Bonar Law's, the latter's discontent was broadcast to the former, compounding Lloyd George's issues for the public, and to some extent, serving to ostracise him from his own government. Indeed, throughout editions of *The Times*, discussion of the upcoming Carlton Club meeting, the Newport by-election and the coalition's future were starred next to information about the Turkish crisis. Therefore, the issue of coalition relations would be a common theme running through the minds of Conservative coalition members, and when the Newport by-election hastened discussions of coalition integrity and importance, these issues were brought to a head and impacted upon the ultimate decision to quit.

Furthermore, the fact that the Carlton Club meeting was not originally arranged to discuss ending the coalition plays into the importance of the Newport by-election. Indeed, one primary source indicates that the club meeting was specifically scheduled so that, in the expected event that either a Liberal/coalition or Labour candidate would win, this would be used as an argument to further bolster defence of the Coalition.[66] Thus, the meeting was originally set up by pro-coalitionists with the aim of constitution of the

---

[65] K. Morgan, 'David Lloyd George' in J. Mackintosh (ed.) *British Prime Ministers in the Twentieth Century: Balfour to Chamberlain* (London, 1977) p.155

[66] Anon. 'Before and After The British Election' *Advocate of Peace Through Justice*, 84 (1922) pp.430-431

alliance, and so the unexpected result of the by-election usurped this in favour of the anti-coalitionist members of the conservatives. This helps to further show Newport's significance, as it drastically changed the course of the meeting, by influencing opinion going into the meeting and the general tone.

So, the Newport by-election was, by this argument, the direct cause of the fall of the coalition government; it magnified the issues and concerns that were being voiced within the media, the public, and the government. It pointed out to the Conservative Party that the source of these problems – Lloyd George, the state of the coalition, the upset non-coalitionist Conservatives, but ultimately the coalition itself – was perhaps not as crucial as it seemed; that the Conservatives had the strength and ability to separate themselves from the Liberals, end the coalition, 'go it alone', and be rid these problems.

Despite the universal acceptance of the huge significance of the Newport by-election, however, there is enough evidence to query this interpretation. Whilst it would be incredibly difficult – and perhaps fruitless – to argue that the by-election did not impact upon the Carlton Club meeting and thus the ending of the coalition, there is still recourse to argue to lower its importance, both as a massive shock that threw the Conservatives into an anti-coalition fervour, and as an extraordinary event within the larger-scale developments of the time.

One way to query the importance is to look at seemingly inexorable processes that have been at play within British politics during the early twentieth century, and to some extent, before this – namely, the Liberal Party decline and Labour's rise. Following the 'inevitablist' line of argument, it is argued that, amongst other things, the Liberals were ill-fitted to the class system of Britain; that the Capital versus Labour cleavage left them with no position to fill once the Labour Party rose to prominence.[67] The Liberal Party was irreparably damaged after the First World War, due in part to the Asquith/Lloyd George split, but largely to actions before the War, such as the aforementioned Labour rise and poor decisions made by the party.[68] As a result, the Liberal Party was incredibly weak and not much of a contender to Labour at all. Following this, then, they would have been little support for the coalition – only token Liberals remained within the government, and many important members of Lloyd George's cabinet had left during peacetime.[69] And, these few Liberals that were left were part of a party that was hugely declining, and thus little use to the Conservatives. Although in the Newport by-election the Liberals had a respectable 26.2% of the vote, the swing against them of -

---

[67] J.A. Thompson, 'The Historians and the Decline of the Liberal Party', *Albion: A Quarterly Journal Concerned with British Studies 22* (Spring 1990) pp.216-235 and D. Powell, 'The New Liberalism and the Rise of Labour, 1886-1906', *The Historical Journal 29* (June 1986) pp.369-393

[68] R.I., Mckibbin, 'James Ramsay Macdonald and the Problem of the Independence of the Labour Party, 1910-1914', *The Journal of Modern History 42* (June 1970) pp.216-235

[69] K. Morgan, 'Lloyd George's Premiership: A Study in 'Prime Ministerial Government', *The Historical Journal 13* (March 1970) pp.130-157

30.2% puts into perspective the Liberal decline. Whilst it was a coalition Liberal in the previous by-election and an independent in the latter, this can be shown to identify specifically the Liberal weakness, and confirm the notion that the Conservatives were helping the Liberals more than the other way around. Thus the decline of the Liberals, whilst shown in the Newport by-election, was too prevalent and long standing a factor to be represented solely within one local contest, and thus their weak position in and eventual removal from the coalition was 'written in stone' long before the Newport contest – it merely provided a signpost of the end, not necessarily a cause.

Primary sources also serve to provide insight into issues that can also be seen to deprive Newport of some of its importance. They illustrate the specifics of the events and people in the time preceding the Carlton Club decision. For example, *The Times* reported on the discontent of the Unionists on the 12th October.[70] The article explains that Chamberlain's, the Conservative leader, and devout coalitionist, Birmingham speech called not just for co-operation with the Liberals in the coalition, but a full union into a new force in politics. The ramifications of this link to the issues surrounding the Conservatives at the time reinforced and entrenched their worries of losing conservative identity within the coalition, certainly playing a large part in anti-coalitionist sentiments of the Conservatives and enforcing the idea of

---

[70] *The Times*, 12th October 1922

separation. Furthermore, this would have given rise to a fall in confidence of Chamberlain as he would have seemed out of touch with his party; thus, when he made his case (a case on which the future of the coalition rested heavily) at the Carlton Club, his previous action would have had a negative impact on the reception of his views, further damaging the coalition.[71]

Furthermore, the by-election itself may not have been significant as it may not have necessarily reflected national trends – the result may have simply been decided by factors relevant to the contest. The fact that Labour was winning seats in neighbouring constituencies hints towards their popularity and dominance in the area, as well as the rest of Wales, and thus in this regard their loss in Newport seems a freak occurrence. This could be explained by the specifics of the election itself. Newspapers reported the Labour campaign was based around opposition and criticism of the coalition, using this as a popular issue to rally the public under Labour's banner.[72] However, whilst this was a popular opinion, it did nothing to present an argument against the other two candidates, who were anti-coalition by their independent nature. Thus, not only did Labour not present a unique or differing argument from the other parties, but this also vastly reduced the argument Labour had against their opponents - opponents who had many criticisms and arguments to pose against the socialist party. Thus, Labour was particularly weak in this election at odds to their

---

[71] *The Financial Times*, 20th October 1922
[72] *The Times*, 7th October 1922

performance around Britain and in wales, highlighting the fact that, in this regard, the Conservatives may not have been particularly strong. The fact that Labour managed to get into government in 1923 further illustrates this; they were strong, despite the Conservative win in Newport.

It cannot be argued that the Newport 1922 by-election was insignificant in the fall of the coalition government. It provided the Conservative Party with the push they needed to separate themselves from the faltering Liberal Party and the increasingly fractious coalition in which they worked together. Furthermore, it provided an insight not only into the machinations of local government but also the issues that wracked political life as a whole, and how these were relayed at a local scale and then utilised in the macro, larger scale.

However, it is important not to reduce such long-spanning (both temporally and spatially) processes down to one by-election – coalition discontent was strong in both the public and political spheres, and without the push of the by-election, the coalition would have almost definitely fallen soon afterwards anyway – perhaps even in the Carlton Club meeting, regardless of the by-election. In addition, in many respects the by-election did not indicate the overarching developments that the Conservatives felt it did – it was one single election subject to the influences upon it that could have skewed the outcome in many different ways.

JOHN AULT

KILMARNOCK: 1933
THOMAS WOWK

The Great Depression of the 1930s played a vital role in shaping both national and local aspects of British politics. Rising unemployment, reaching 3.5 million in the UK by 1932, and a decline in trade and industry resulted in the British electorate becoming more volatile towards the mainstream political parties. This economic climate consequently fractured international politics with world peace and the disarmament campaigns of the 1930s struggling to be carried out by the League of Nations. The by-election contest at Kilmarnock in 1933 can be seen to have revolved around such major issues; the micro politics of local economic stability reflected the macro environment of the British government trying to resolve the crisis on a national scale. The election result saw National Labour's candidate K.M Lindsay win. As a result, it could be suggested the National Government's performance since 1931 secured the approval of the Kilmarnock electorate. However, the result still remains one of lowest ever percentage of votes to win an election, securing just 34.8% of constituency support.[73] This essay will examine the reasons why this National Labour victory was so slim. One reason which will be considered is the Labour Party's divisions during this period and how this is identified at Kilmarnock in 1933. Further explanations as to why the Kilmarnock by-election was so close will be analysed, including the emergence of Scottish nationalism, the decline of Liberalism in Scotland by 1930s and the absence of a Unionist candidate at Kilmarnock. What will be identified is the monumental role in which the UK's economic instability of the 1930s dictated local politics.

The heavily contested Labour vote at Kilmarnock in 1933 may be indicative of internal Labour conflicts during the 1930s. The election itself saw three separate Labour candidates stand: National Labour, official Labour and even Independent Labour. This division relates to the Labour split following the 1931 election, when Ramsay MacDonald entered the National Government to deal with the economic crisis from a bi-partisan stance.[74] As a result, it can be argued the fractured nature of Labour during the 1930s, a macro development as a consequence of the national economic turmoil, is portrayed by the Kilmarnock

---

[73] F.W.S Craig, *British Parliamentary Election Results 1918-1949*, 3rd Ed.,(Surrey, 1983) p.616

[74] A. Thorpe, *A History of the British Labour Party*, 3rd Ed., (London, 2008) p.84

by-election on a local level through the multitude of Labour candidates.

Kilmarnock in 1933 can also been seen as a referendum on the National Governments' economic performance. The result highlights that 83.1% of the local electorate were tightly divided between three Labour candidates who stood separately because of their differing approaches to the economic crisis.[75] The Glasgow Herald just two days before the election acknowledged that the contest would revolve around the National Government, being a "for or against" vote on whether the electorate commended its economic performance since 1931.[76] The voters at Kilmarnock were therefore required to make a choice between which party looked most likely to fix the national crisis in the local context. Consequently, the local issues of the Kilmarnock by-election in 1933 can be seen to have been directly linked to the economic instability of the 1930s, with the local voters assessing the performance of the National Government.

The divisions of the Labour vote at Kilmarnock in 1933 can be argued to indirectly reflect the poor performance of the National Government regarding foreign policy. International diplomacy, becoming more volatile due the Great Depression, resulted in the League of Nations and Britain as a major member struggling to safeguard global peace. For example, by 1933 the British handling

---

[75] F.W.S Craig, *British Parliamentary Election Results 1918-1949*, 3*rd* Ed.,(Surrey, 1983) p.616
[76] *The Glasgow Herald,* 1st November 1933

of the Manchurian Crisis had begun to face criticism from the League. This criticism was specifically directed at the speed of the response from the Lytton Commission, set up to address the Manchurian Crisis by the British.[77] Furthermore, the failure of the Disarmament Conference in October 1933, with Germany withdrawing from the meeting and the League of Nations simultaneously, also represented a failure on behalf of the British government, which supported global disarmament. The Glasgow Herald in October 1933 highlighted how Britain's foreign policy had begun to be questioned, dividing public opinion regarding its popularity.[78] With National Labour being seen as the head of the National Government and a Peace Ballot poll in October 1933 recording 57% support for unilateral disarmament, the divided support for the party at Kilmarnock can represent a protest vote against National Labour's handling of foreign policy in that year.[79] Here then, the macro politics of foreign policy, hindered greatly by the economic instability of the 1930s, helped shaped the conditions of this micro by-election.

Kilmarnock then neatly identifies, in the case of the Labour Party, how the macro issue of the Great Depression influenced the way in which the micro electorate voted. Some would suggest the late withdrawal of the National Labour candidate, Sir Alexander Mackenzie Livingston, in early October 1933 may have affected

---

[77] *The Times Newspaper,* 18th January 1933
[78] *The Glasgow Herald,* 5th October 1933
[79] M. Ceadel, 'The First British Referendum: The Peace Ballot 1934-35', *The English Historical Review, 95, 377* (Oct., 1980) p.810-839

the voting loyalties of the Kilmarnock election.[80] However, national economic conditions were far more likely to have affected the local electorate than Mackenzie's withdrawal. The Labour Party since the dawn of the Great Depression had faced national internal divisions which Kilmarnock reflects accurately. Linked to the Great Depression is the decline in international relations. As a consequence, Britain's foreign policy performance would face difficulties and the local newspapers of Kilmarnock highlight the voter's consideration of this factor before voting. Here then, the state of the world economy and its knock-on effects on international diplomacy, being the macro environment of British politics, can be viewed as being considered by the Kilmarnock voters in this micro election.

Another consequence of the economic turmoil existing around The Kilmarnock by-election of 1933 was the growth in popularity for Scottish Nationalism. The seat before this election had never had a nationalist candidate compete. But with MacEwen securing 16.9% of the vote at Kilmarnock, the election confirms the support for a nationalist agenda.[81] This electoral success can be directly associated to the economic turmoil of the 1930s. Just days before the election, the *Glasgow Herald* stated how the Scottish Nationals could secure the "protest vote", with the decline in the British economy forcing the electorate to reconsider the

---

[80] *The Glasgow Herald,* 4th October 1933
[81] F.W.S Craig, *British Parliamentary Election Results 1918-1949, 3rd Ed.,*(Surrey, 1983) p.616

competence of the mainstream political parties.[82] MacEwen himself acknowledges how the "economic upheaval" of the current time helped the nationalist voice elevate to a more potent tone.[83] Contemporary politics still portrays this link between rises in nationalist agendas with a decline in economic conditions; *The Scotsman Today* emphasized the growing strength of Scottish independence thanks to Britain's reduced credit rating.[84] When one considers that on average 20% of the Scottish population were unemployed in the 1930's, the success of the Scottish Nationalist Party in this election through economic protest voting can be better understood.[85] Kilmarnock under such analysis appears to illustrate the growing discontent of the micro electorate over the macro issue of the Great Depression, with Scottish nationalism benefiting as a consequence.

Despite this success, the Kilmarnock exaggerates the electoral support for Scottish nationalism in the 1930's. It cannot be taken away from the Scottish Nationalist Party that by securing 16.9% of the popular vote they had secured some success for a minor party. However, the result does distort the extent of nationalist support across Scotland. The Municipal Elections across Scotland on the 8th November, just five days after the Kilmarnock

---

[82] *The Glasgow Herald*, 1st November 1933
[83] Sir A. M. MacEwen, *The Thistle and the Rose: Scotland's Problems To-day*, (Edinburgh, 1932) p.1
[84] *The Scotsmen Today*, 24th February 2013
[85] W. W. Knox, *A History of the Scottish People: Summary of Economy and Society in Scotland 1840-1940*

result, had not one seat contested by a Scottish National candidate.[86] A party which could not compete on a grass roots level to represent nationalist views hardly represents a party with national support. Such evidence helps portray the more realistic picture of Scottish nationalist support at that current time, sporadic and incoherent.

Alternate by-elections around 1933 can further illustrate the lack of support for Scottish Nationalism. The Fife Eastern by-election in that same year saw a National Party of Scotland candidate only secure 3.6% of the vote.[87] In 1935, Kilmarnock went to the vote and the Scottish National Party would only secure 6.2% of the vote.[88] That same year, the Nationalists secured just 7.8% of the vote in Dunbartonshire.[89] Peter Lynch's research into the history of the Scottish National Party reveals how despite the advancements of self-determination in the 1920's such as Irish independence, Scottish Home Rule failed to secure a "positive political climate".[90] Such evidence helps more accurately portray the minimal support for Scottish nationalism during the early years of the 1930's.

The lack of coherent electoral success for the Scottish

---

[86] *The Glasgow Herald,* 8th November 1933
[87] F.W.S Craig, *British Parliamentary Election Results 1918-1949,* 3rd Ed.,(Surrey, 1983) p.616
[88] *Ibid.* p.616.
[89] *Ibid.* p.622.
[90] P. Lynch, *SNP, The History of the Scottish National Party,* (Cardiff, 2002) p.592

Nationalist Party despite the Kilmarnock by-election result can be better understood when its internal divisions are highlighted. The issue of Scottish nationalism during the 1920's and 1930's was that of direction; whether to pursue independence, fundamentalists, or to adopt a more practical approach through devolution, gradualists. Lynch argues the very nature of the party created soon after Kilmarnock, the Scottish Nationalist Party, made it "born into difficult times", with the party being fractured over "strategy, ideology and constitutional goals".[91] Because of this electoral struggle in the 1930's some, such as Ewen A. Cameron, have questioned whether the Scottish Nationalists should have contested elections.[92] Such internal difficulties over direction would cost them electorally, seen through their inconsistent levels of support across Scotland; an electorate find it hard to vote for party which can't convincingly portray its agenda.

Kilmarnock then can be seen to offer a deceptive picture of the state of Scottish nationalism in 1933. The result itself for MacEwen and the soon to be Scottish Nationalist Party can be deemed a short-term success. MacEwen suggested there had been a "revival in national consciousness" and the Kilmarnock result could exemplify such a revival.[93] This in turn reflected, as

---

[91] P. Lynch, *SNP, The History of the Scottish National Party,* (Cardiff, 2002) p.42
[92] E. A. Cameron *Impaled Upon a Thistle: Scotland since 1880,* (Edinburgh, 2010) p.169
[93] Sir A. M. MacEwen, *The Thistle and the Rose: Scotland's Problems To-day,* (Edinburgh, 1932) p.1

MacEwen theorized, a "spirit of restlessness and discontent" with British mainstream political parties which in turn allowed the Scottish Nationals to gain significant support.[94] However, this interpretation lacks any serious validity to its argument. The fact that the Scottish Nationalist Party only had 1,200 members in 1945, 11 years after its creation, illustrates the lack of widespread support for the nationalist agenda in Scotland.[95] Consequently, the economic climate surrounding Kilmarnock in 1933 can be accredited as the main reason for MacEwen's success, appearing as candidate for a protest vote against the National Government's economic performance, and not a signifier of coherent support for Scottish nationalism in the 1930s.

The decline of the Liberal Party by the 1930's in Scotland, whom previously were Home Rule specialists in British politics, also offers some explanation as to why the Scottish Nationals gained such support in Kilmarnock in 1933. Post-War Liberalism no longer convincingly captured the Scottish electorate, exemplified by the struggles of their leader, Herbert Asquith, in unsuccessfully competing East Fife, 1918 and Paisley in 1924.[96] This lack of a convincing agenda in the eyes of the electorate is highlighted by the fact that no candidate for the Liberals even

---

[94] Sir A. M. MacEwen, *The Thistle and the Rose: Scotland's Problems To-day*, (Edinburgh, 1932) p.1
[95] P. Lynch, *SNP, The History of the Scottish National Party*, (Cardiff, 2002) p.592
[96] E. A. Cameron *Impaled Upon a Thistle: Scotland since 1880*, (Edinburgh, 2010) p.154

contested Kilmarnock in 1933 and hadn't previously contested here since 1929 despite two opportunities.[97] Consequently, MacEwen was given an opportunity to usurp the support of the liberal electorate in Kilmarnock, a party which often sympathised with nationalist policies. *The Glasgow Herald* the day before the election acknowledged as such by suggesting MacEwen would be able to secure "Liberal Votes".[98] It can therefore be suggested the absence of a Liberal Party on macro level allowed the Scottish Nationals to usurp nationalist support and intensify their electoral gain in Kilmarnock 1933 on a micro platform.

The Liberal absence at Kilmarnock acts a fitting portrayal of the party's condition nationally. Scotland was no longer a Celtic Fringe for Liberalism to survive in. Just two years previous in the 1931 General Election, the Liberals had only managed to secure 8.6% of the Scottish vote.[99] Part of this poor display from the Liberals is due to their internal divisions, as the Glasgow Herald indicates, with the National Liberals securing 35 seats and being part of the National Coalition.[100] This lack of success electorally is accredited to financial difficulties, with the Scottish Liberal Federation revenue only accounting for "three quarter of the annual

---

[97] F.W.S Craig, *British Parliamentary Election Results 1918-1949, 3rd Ed.*,(Surrey, 1983) p.616
[98] *The Glasgow Herald*, 1st November 1933
[99] F. W. S. Craig, *British Electoral Facts, 1832-1987*, (Dartmouth, 1989) Tables 1.22-27
[100] *The Glasgow Herald*, 28th October 1931

expenditure".[101] With tight finances it is no surprise the Liberals failed to offer coherent electoral campaigning in Scotland during the 1930's, reflected aptly by the absence of Liberal candidate in Kilmarnock, 1933.

The decline of Liberalism in Britain by the 1930's also helped the Labour Party in Scotland, illustrated in turn at Kilmarnock on a micro level. The Franchise Act of 1918 relocated many Scottish seats from agricultural areas to urbanized populations resulting in Celtic Liberal strongholds being relocated to Labour industrialised seats.[102] This in turn represents the shifting nature of support from the Liberals to Labour in Scotland, as the "working-class Liberal moved comfortably to Labour".[103] However, this newly gained support can be argued to have been severely tested by Labour split of 1931. The election clearly dominated by economic factors reduced Scottish Labour to just seven seats.[104] Consequently, whilst more of the Scottish electorate became sympathetic to Labour appeals, the state of Britain's' economy would dictate the extent of this new found Labour support. So, despite the potential for Labour gains due to Liberal decline by the 1930's, The Kilmarnock by-election of 1933 emphasises the importance of Britain's' economy in influencing

---

[101] I. G. C. Hutchison, *Scottish Politics in the Twentieth Century* (Basingstoke, 2001) p.37
[102] *Ibid.* p.30
[103] *Ibid.* p. 41
[104] E. A. Cameron, *Impaled Upon a Thistle: Scotland Since 1880,* (Edinburgh, 2010) p.161

voting rather than the decline in Liberal support.

What the Kilmarnock by-election of 1933 doesn't identify is the extent of conservative support in Scotland during the 1930s. Despite a 50% cut in revenue for the Scottish Unionist Association, conservative support would still remain considerable in Scotland.[105] Once again, the importance of the national economics on localized politics during the 1930s can be clearly identified, with the macro condition of Britain's economy dictating the local condition Conservative organisational structure. The support for Conservatives during this period had previously is identified by the 1931 UK General Election, winning 50 seats out of a possible 74.[106] Much of this success can be argued to be as a result of the party modernizing in terms organisation and structure. Hutchinson highlights such developments, with electoral strategy looking to target the weakening Liberal vote as noted above, the organization incorporating the newly franchised female electorate and greater consideration for younger voters helping to increase the party's support.[107] Such research then highlights the importance of party organisation on a local level to help secure national success in British politics.

Despite this Conservative presence in Scotland during the

---

[105] I. G. C. Hutchison, *Scottish Politics in the Twentieth Century* (Basingstoke, 2001) p.44
[106] Stuart Ball, *The Conservative Party and British Politics 1902-1951*, (Harlow, 1995) p.86
[107] I. G. C. Hutchison, *Scottish Politics in the Twentieth Century* (Basingstoke, 2001)

1930s, Kilmarnock seat never became a Conservative stronghold. Economic factors hindered its ability to secure the seat. The Conservatives last secured the constituency as far back as 1924.[108] This lack of Conservative support can be accredited to the industrial nature of the constituency, with its main industries being textiles and engineering. As touched on above, it would be the Labour party who would find the majority support in these industrialised districts. Furthermore, the inability of the Conservatives in Scotland to deal with the agricultural crisis of the 1930s, a direct consequence of the nation's economic turmoil, can be indirectly linked to have hindered the Conservative vote on a local level. Kilmarnock, driven by the textile industry and its consequent links to agriculture, would view this lack of success with dealing with the agricultural crisis by consistently resisting a Conservative seat. Once again, economic conditions in local politics, influenced by the national crisis of the 1930s, dictated the way in which the Kilmarnock electorate voted.

Overall, Kilmarnock in 1933 identifies the central importance of economics in shaping both the macro and micro elements of British politics at this time. The Labour party, clearly divided over economic policy since 1931, is portrayed accurately at Kilmarnock on a micro level. The vote in turn can be seen to reflect a referendum on the National government's recent foreign policy performance, now facing greater difficulty due the economic

---

[108] F.W.S Craig, *British Parliamentary Election Results 1918-1949*, 3rd Ed., (Surrey, 1983) p.616

depression. The success of Scottish nationalism at Kilmarnock in 1933, although an inaccurate portrayal of its strength of support in Scotland, reveals the importance of the nation's economic instability and how this facilitated a protest vote on a micro scale. The absence of a Liberal candidate at Kilmarnock identifies not only the decline of liberalism in Scotland's Celtic Fringe but on a national scale too. The absence of a Conservative at Kilmarnock does not allow for the strength of conservatism in Scotland to be acknowledged during this period but it does allow for the importance of local economics constituting a lack of support for the Conservatives in this constituency. Both national and local issues revolved around the economic crisis and this would only change after World War Two and greater consideration for the social condition of Britain.

CARMARTHEN: 1966
MILES FOWLER

On 14th July 1966, Gwynfor Evans, a long-standing advocate of Welsh nationalism, ran for and subsequently won the seat of Carmarthen in Parliament. It was arguably a surprise victory for Plaid Cymru and a great step forward towards Welsh devolution. The by-election was brought about by the death of former Liberal icon and Welsh radical Megan Lloyd George, the then-Labour representative for Carmarthen and the daughter of former Prime Minister David Lloyd George. She had held the seat from 1957 to 1966. The victory for Evans was no doubt a shock to many; just four months earlier in the General Election, Megan Lloyd George had once again maintained her seat while Evans came third, polling 7,416 votes compared to her 21,221.[109] In his autobiography Evans describes this surprise with a story he had

---

[109] R. Kimber, *UK General Election Results March 1966*

heard where a friend called in at a newsagent's at seven in the morning of the 14th July; "'Have you heard Gwynfor Evans has gone in at Carmarthen?'", he asked the woman who kept the shop. "Poor dab," she replied, thinking no doubt of St. David's mental hospital, "I hope they won't have to keep him in too long."'[110] What then, did this surprise victory mean for UK Politics? The by-election went on to encourage an increase in support for Plaid Cymru in the Rhondda West and Caerphilly by-elections in 1967 and 1968 respectively, but in a wider context, how significant is this by-election? It is this question that will be addressed throughout this chapter, by looking at how the historical, political and social landscape of Carmarthen had an effect on the by-election, how Megan Lloyd George, herself, affected the outcome, and Gwynfor Evans' perspective on his victory.

This history of Carmarthen as a town has a very significant role in understanding why both Megan Lloyd George and Gwynfor Evans were popular politicians in the area. It is often said that Carmarthen is the oldest town in Wales; J.G. Edwards' article on the town's early history goes back as far as 1284 and the Statute of Rhuddlan that brought Wales under the governmental rule of England. The statute also subjected Wales to new borders and counties; Wales was split into two districts, North and West Wales, with Carmarthen making up part of the West district.[111]

---

[110] G. Evans, *For the Sake of Wales,* Second Edition, (Wales, 1996) pp.174-175
[111] J. G. Edwards, 'The Early History of the Counties of Carmarthen and Cardigan', *The English Historical Review,* (1916) p.90

Carmarthen's history dates back much further than this however, as Edwards also draws upon the pre-Magna Carta days and the reign of Henry I, who seized Carmarthen and built a castle there.[112] This far-reaching history of Carmarthen gives it a sense of historical grounding and identity that is built around the subjugation of Wales in the latter half of the medieval period. As such, nationalist feelings and beliefs that were present in Plaid Cymru could be said to be the next development in a long history of struggle against English government, and not just the product of a twentieth-century ideology.

The extensive history also creates a somewhat romanticised relationship between the town and the people based on traditions. This is reflected in the fact that Carmarthen is also one of the few areas in South West Wales that has a majority Welsh speaking population. The town also has a lot to offer in terms of archaeology and geology, making the town's composition and make-up a sense of pride not only for its inhabitants, but also an area of interest for those interested in Wales' long history.

Despite being a county town, Carmarthen is something of a rural market place (the town's population was estimated to be just 13,760 in the 2001 census). The size of the town would also likely have an effect on the nationalism in the area; a smaller town would breed a greater feeling of community and togetherness, brought

---

[112] J. G. Edwards, 'The Early History of the Counties of Carmarthen and Cardigan', *The English Historical Review,* (1916) pp.90-91

about through a closely knit settlement, an attribute that is found in Plaid Cymru and Gwynfor Evans' political beliefs, as will be seen later.

Carmarthen's history and geography thus shows us how nationalism was likely to thrive in the town, but one of the main factors in the growth of nationalism is mostly down to the political situation of the area. The relationship between Carmarthen and the Lloyd George family was certainly close; David Lloyd George was made an honorary Freeman for the town in 1923, and as previously mentioned, his daughter Megan held the seat in Parliament from 1957, where she beat Plaid Cymru candidate Jennie Eirian Davies by 20,000 votes, and held this seat until her death in 1966.[113] Paul Ward cites this popularity for not just Megan, but for the entire Lloyd George family to 'a particular and powerful version of Welshness associated with nonconformity' which resonated with not only rural Wales, but also the southern industrial communities.[114] In fact, Ward even goes on to say that the 'political pluralism' demonstrated through this nonconformity could strengthen the Empire 'allowing the expression of difference within the unity'.[115] The number of votes Megan Lloyd George won by and the fact that she was re-elected three times more (in 1959, 1964 and March 1966) proves she was a popular candidate. Her obituaries paint a similar picture; as well as likening her

---

[113] *The Evening Times,* 19th February 1957
[114] P. Ward, *Unionism in the United Kingdom 1918-1974,* (Basingstoke, 2005) p.74
[115] *Ibid* p.80

attitude to that of her father, Dingle Foot retells a story from her campaign for Carmarthen where "every meeting was packed to the doors."[116] She is also accredited to being the President of the Parliament for Wales campaign, and is described as a 'Welsh Radical'.[117] Of course, the nature of obituaries as a source means it is vital to be aware that they focus on the positive aspects of one's life and not the negative. Consequently, this means Megan Lloyd George's obituary must be looked at with this in mind. Nonetheless, to her constituents, she was not a Labour candidate, or a Liberal; she was a Lloyd George.

Considering her interest in Welsh devolution, Megan Lloyd George's shift towards Labour could be seen as a strategic move; the centralisation of the Liberals, and the loss of the more Radical party members left her in a less than ideal position in staying with her historic party. Coupled with Megan's loss of her seat at Anglesey and her desire to return to the House of Commons meant that a shift towards Labour would leave her in a better political position. She was famously quoted to have retorted with 'I'm not of a retiring age nor of a retiring disposition' when asked by a reporter if her loss at Anglesey and subsequent stepping down as Deputy Liberal Party Leader meant she was retiring.[118] Mervyn Jones writes in his biography of Megan Lloyd George that despite their hostility to devolution, Labour had a 'comradely alliance with

---

[116] *The Times*, 17th May 1966
[117] *Ibid.*
[118] M. Jones, *A Radical Life: The Biography of Megan Lloyd George*, (London, 1991) p. 235

the whole British working class.'[119] Particularly in Wales this was the case; Plaid Cymru's opposition was largely against the Labour Party because of their working class credentials. Therefore, Megan's affiliation with Labour would allow her to use her status as a Welsh radical to gain the support of the already supportive working class, which would allow her to establish a platform to push for Welsh self-government. In contrast, J. Graham Jones writes that this was easier said than done though; he thinks she 'may have found herself somewhat hamstrung, missing her former freedom as the highly independent backbench Liberal member for Angelsey' and struggled with 'her new party's reluctance to embrace a worthwhile measure of devolution for Wales.'[120] Certainly, as a collective party, Labour's interest in Welsh devolution was passive at best at this point, but that did not deter Megan from joining the party ranks. Welsh devolution was the goal to be achieved, but her move to Labour was because of a dissatisfaction of what the Liberal Party had become, leading to her disinterest in the party. She is noted to have said 'The Liberal Party left me, not the other way about' when asked if she would return to the party in the case of a revival.[121] She also saw the opportunity to gain the working class support once again through joining Labour. She could use the reputation of Labour as a

---

[119] M. Jones, *A Radical Life: The Biography of Megan Lloyd George*, (London, 1991) p. 233
[120] J. G. Jones, 'A Breach in the Family', *The Journal of Liberal Democrat History*, (1999) p.36
[121] M. Jones, *A Radical Life: The Biography of Megan Lloyd George*, (London, 1991) p.249

working class party to solidify this demographic. Indeed this move paid off in terms of her success; Labour's political dominance in Wales allowed her to maintain her seat in Carmarthen until her death in 1966. In 1959, the party received 47.89% of the votes in Carmarthen, in 1964, they won 45.46% and in 1966, it was 45.46% of the votes.[122]

According to Gareth Evans, the beginning of Labour's stranglehold on Wales came in the General Election after the Second World War with the party's landslide victory, which he attributes to 'social solidarity generated by years of military conflict, industrial stagnation and economic depression.'[123] The mix of a failing economy and industry in Wales helped keep Labour alive, especially during the economic boom of the Conservative government during the 1950s. As has been established, Megan Lloyd George used this situation to push for Welsh devolution. She was the President for the Parliament for Wales Campaign, which ran from 1950 to 1956 and gained 250,000 signatures, a truly substantial amount, despite its rejection by the Conservative government. As Laura McAllister claims, despite the impact of the campaign on the government was minimal, having 'failed to mobilise widespread popular support', it was still effective in fuelling nationalism in Wales, with her subsequently winning the 1957 by-election in Carmarthen, which

---

[122] R. Kimber, *General Election Results October 1959*, R. Kimber, *General Election Results October 1964*, R. Kimber, *General Election Results March 1966*
[123] D. G. Evans, *A History of Wales 1906-2000*, (Wales, 2000) p.211

was then of course won by Gwynfor Evans in 1966.[124] If Megan Lloyd George's success can be put down to her popularity as the daughter of the former Welsh Prime Minister and because Wales was such a Labour stronghold in comparison to Plaid Cymru, how then did Evans win the Carmarthen by-election by being part of what was essentially a fringe party?

In 1979, Denis Balsom wrote that Plaid Cymru is 'an amalgam of conservatism and radicalism, the precise mixture of which had varied over its lifespan as a party.'[125] Balsom sees Plaid Cymru becoming a party in its own right after Evans' victory in 1966, and so has failed to address the party's acceptance of left-wing ideology. Whilst one might traditionally think of nationalism to be a more right-wing ideology, especially in post-war Europe, Alan Sandry actually argues that socialist ideals were the basis of the political programme of Plaid Cymru.[126] With much of Wales' industry based around typically working class jobs, such as mining and manufacturing, left wing ideology was more likely to take root and subsequently thrive. Therefore, as a party that is arguably supposed to represent Wales' interests, Plaid Cymru would have to appeal to these beliefs to win over support. That is not to say that Plaid Cymru were advocating some form of *national socialism* with their ideology, but rather they demonstrated an awareness of

---

[124] L. McAllister, *Plaid Cymru: The Emergence of a Political Party*, (Bridgend, 2001) pp.99-100
[125] D. Balsom, 'Plaid Cymru: the Welsh National Party' in H.M. Drucker (ed.) *Multi-Party Britain*, (Basingstoke, 1979) p.131
[126] A. Sandry, *Plaid Cymru: An Ideological Analysis,* (Wales, 2011) p.102.

popular politics in Wales that encompassed support for both Labour and the nationalist agenda. To take the issue of employment as an example, Evans' *Black Book* shows how he extensively questioned the President of the Board of Trade on what measures were being taken to increase employment in Carmarthen.[127] This is just one example from the 45-page booklet filled solely with questions that Evans asked during his time in the House of Commons. Other examples concern the closure of mines, industrial training, factories, education, as well as the Welsh language, showing how Evans was incorporating both the concerns of the working class with his own goal towards better representation for the Welsh, and ultimately devolution. The question that then arises is whether Plaid Cymru and Evans considered themselves to be socialist. Socialism seeks to rise above concerns of ethnicity or nation, whereas nationalism seeks to promote differences of a particular set of people (in this case Wales). If Plaid Cymru did in fact consider themselves to be socialist, how would they be different from their main opposition, the Labour Party?

It is known that Evans did not see himself as socialist because socialism would always be associated with Labour[128]. For members of the Plaid Cymru, Labour was seen as their main opposition 'for the hearts and minds of the Welsh electorate'; as such, to determine that Plaid Cymru was socialist would imply a

---

[127] G. Evans, *Black Paper on Wales on 1967,* (Cardiff, 1967) p.12
[128] A. Sandry, *Plaid Cymru: An Ideological Analysis,* (Wales, 2011) p.105

connection between the two parties.[129] This does not prove that neither Evans nor Plaid Cymru as a whole did not show concern for the issues affecting the Welsh working class though. In 1968, Evans published a booklet titled *Welsh Nationalist Aims* which, despite covering nationalist topics as the 'Place of National Community' or 'A Confraternity of Nations', still had many socialist themes that ran through it; Evans also discusses 'The evils of concentrating power in one man or in a group have been demonstrated in more than one country' and how the State destroys communities, religious, social or otherwise.[130] To conclude, Evans even writes that 'a root cause of the decay of the Welsh nation has been the denationalising of the Labour movement...whoever is to bring her salvation must fuse the power of the labour and nationalist movements in one creative force'.[131] Here we see an acknowledgement of Labour's efforts for the benefit of the Welsh working class, as well as a confrontation with their attempts at denationalisation. It is the former acknowledgement that Evans wishes Plaid Cymru to take on board. It is in this way that Plaid Cymru were more than a party that just replicated the ideology of Labour in Wales, but adopted left-wing ideals and at the same time fitted to them to their mould of nationalism.

Of course, this is to say that Plaid Cymru adopted left-wing ideas to gain votes and support. How well did this reflect in their

---

[129] A. Sandry, *Plaid Cymru: An Ideological Analysis*, (Wales, 2011) p.105
[130] G. Evans, *Welsh Nationalist Aims*, (Carmarthen, 1968) pp.3,7,9
[131] *Ibid.* p.19

votes? By looking at the statistics of Plaid Cymru's results in Carmarthen for the General Elections of October 1959 and March 1966, their votes still sit under 10,000 (the highest number of votes received was 7,416 in 1966). Bearing in mind these results are from Carmarthen as well, one of the more nationalist areas of Wales, it makes sense to compare them to another seat in Wales. In the town of Cardigan in Mid-Wales, votes for Plaid Cymru stayed between 2,500 and 3,500 between 1959 and 1966, showing that while it may seem that Plaid Cymru adopted left-wing policies to swing votes for them, it was still not enough to establish themselves as legitimate competition for Labour. In fact, it wasn't until Evans won in October of 1966 that Labour began to be concerned with the opposition Plaid Cymru posed to them, and even that was short-lived, when by the next General Election in 1970, Evans had lost his seat to the Labour candidate (later to become part of the Social Democratic Party) Gwynoro Jones. An interesting contrast is exhibited in the comparison between votes from Carmarthen and votes from Cardigan; while Plaid Cymru's votes in Carmarthen were higher, they were not as consistent as those from Cardigan. Two possible deductions can be made from this; first of all, it illustrates the choice that Plaid Cymru could exert their support on a constituency that was capable of gaining high votes, or on a constituency that was gaining consistent votes. Secondly, it makes us question why Plaid Cymru gained more votes in March 1966. Support for Plaid Cymru in Carmarthen had been slowly increasing as a legitimate platform to tackle the issue of self-government. This was not so much because of dissatisfaction with Megan Lloyd George's leadership as it was about dissatisfaction with Labour as a party. As a whole, Labour opposed devolution for Wales, creating a difficult position for Megan to exert radicalism into mainstream politics, despite the support she gained from joining the party. A fringe party such as Plaid Cymru might just have been the answer for a better chance at achieving this. A smaller base of like-minded supporters would mean less conflict internally, which could then be extended and expanded upon. The passing of Megan Lloyd George certainly came as a shock considering she was fit to run for a seat in May of that year. Her death left a gap to be filled by another Welsh radical, namely Gwynfor Evans.

How did Gwynfor Evans perceive his victory in July 1996 then? As previously mentioned, Evans winning Carmarthen in 1966 was seen as a shock victory to many people, since he had performed relatively poorly in March of that year. After all, in the previous election, Evans gained 7,416 votes, in comparison to Megan Lloyd George's 21,221. In *The Times* coverage of the victory, it is described as 'a shock' for Labour, after having held the seat for nine years.[132] Even Evans himself writes about how he couldn't believe he had won ('Outside the Guild Hall in Carmarthen Elwyn Roberts was waiting for me. He had just come out of the count with the news that I was in. Though he swore this

---

[132] *The Times*, 16th July 1966

was the Gospel truth, I just couldn't believe it').[133] What is of particular interest here is that in his victory speech, Evans speaks more about Wales as a whole, rather than Carmarthen. For instance, he says his win has 'transformed utterly and in an instant, the prospects of the Welsh nation'.[134] Likewise, to go back to his 1967 *Black Book*, many of the questions he poses concern Wales as a whole; 'Mr. Gwynfor Evans asked the Secretary of State for Wales what percentage of the total United Kingdom expenditure on motorways and dual carriageways was spent in Wales in each year from 1960 to 1965'.[135] Evans seems to be overly ambitious in thinking that this is the beginning of a process towards devolution. He saw himself as a representative for all of Wales, rather than just Carmarthen. This could explain why Labour felt competition from Plaid Cymru despite having only won one seat; Evans spoke as if it was on the behalf of all of Wales' constituencies, effectively stepping on Labour's territory. What more, in both his speech and his autobiography, Evans compares the possible outcomes of this victory to that of the fall of the Bastille, showing how ambitious he was about this victory; he saw it almost as the beginning of a revolution for Wales, deliberately exaggerating the misrepresentation of the country in Parliament.[136] To an extent, he can be forgiven for this, since as the first representative for Plaid

---

[133] G. Evans, *For the Sake of Wales*, (Llandudno, 1996) p.174
[134] G. Evans, *Wales Resurgent*, http://www.youtube.com/watch?v=_ms6JFJqpU0, last accessed 22/03/2013.
[135] G. Evans, *Black Paper on Wales 1967*, (Cardiff, 1967) p.24
[136] G. Evans, *For the Sake of Wales*, (Llandudno, 1996) p.174

Cymru in Parliament, a party whose aim was to represent the whole of Wales, he must have felt a sense of responsibility to represent more than just the Carmarthen constituency in the House of Commons.

In reality, Evans' ambitions were more difficult to achieve than he perceived. His first question to the Prime Minister asked whether he would present a Bill for the establishment of a Parliament with Wales, to which the answer was an immediate and resounding 'No.'[137] He also stated he was uncomfortable at Westminster; 'If Megan Lloyd George was like a fish out of water when not at Westminster, that's how I felt within its walls.'[138] His relationship with Parliament certainly seems to be a complex one; despite his enthusiasm, he felt out of place with the people there. For example, on his first day, while being shown around, he was told by Emrys Hughes (A Member of the Labour Party who represented South Ayrshire) to never sit at the Welsh table in the tea-room because his '"name was mud there"', which makes sense since there would have been so many Labour representatives there.[139] Despite this, he played up to his reputation in Plaid Cymru as a hero of sorts, by trying to represent both his constituency and the Welsh nation as a whole.

To conclude, the 1966 Carmarthen by-election was certainly significant for Plaid Cymru in an immediate sense.

---

[137] G. Evans, *For the Sake of Wales*, (Llandudno, 1996) p.177
[138] *Ibid.* p.180
[139] *Ibid.* p.179

Evans' victory saw increased support for the party within his constituency and in others, illustrated by the significant increase in votes in Rhondda West Caerphilly in 1967 and 1968. It established Plaid Cymru as an effective political party, an issue that was somewhat ambiguous in the years preceding the success in Carmarthen in 1966, at least in the early years of the party. Whilst the party contested parliamentary seats, it had many attributes similar to that of a pressure group; they upheld support the Welsh language and culture and promoted Welsh consciousness.[140] It could be said that they had difficulty establishing a concise ideological identity (although this might seem like too much of a generalisation). They also whole-heartedly backed non-electoral campaigns, such as the 'Parliament for Wales' campaign between 1950 and 1956. The question of whether Plaid Cymru was until this point ever really considered a political party is not to be discussed in detail here however, since it is not of primary concern to the topic.

Megan Lloyd George's influence should not be forgotten either. Despite her affiliation with the Liberal Party, and then with Labour, her reputation as a Lloyd George helped create a voice for nationalism in Wales that worked as a base for Evans and for Plaid Cymru in this area. While politically, Megan and Gwynfor opposed each other, they seemed to have a close personal relationship. Both had had similar political beliefs and were part of

---

[140] D. Balsom, 'Plaid Cymru: the Welsh National Party' in H.M. Drucker (ed.) *Multi-Party Britain*, (Basingstoke, 1979) p.152

the Parliament for Wales Campaign. In 1957, Evans questioned 'why is Lady Megan fighting us if she is seriously in support of any measure of Welsh self-government?'[141] Ultimately, the two were similar in ideology despite their separate parties. Her death was a big blow to the Welsh cause, but it allowed Gwynfor to step up and represent nationalism under its new banner - Plaid Cymru.

Evans' victory was certainly hugely significant for Plaid Cymru. As shown, it established them as a credible party in Wales which saw an increase in support. It was indeed a significant step forward for Welsh devolution, and to some extent, undermined Labour's stranglehold on post-war Welsh politics. However, Plaid Cymru's relationship with the Labour Party in Wales is more complicated. While the party benefitted from Evans' victory, in comparison to Labour's success in Wales, it seems somewhat minimal. Wales was still very much a Labour stronghold, and despite Evans winning Carmarthen, it was lost again to Gwynoro Jones just four years later. Similarly, while Carmarthen spawned the success of Rhondda West and Caerphilly, Plaid Cymru still did not win these by-elections, they still came second to Labour. What is notable about the results from these by-elections though is that the percentage of votes received by Plaid Cymru is higher than in Carmarthen. The number of votes between Plaid Cymru and Labour in these seats is also closer than it is in Carmarthen, implying that this constituency was not as supportive of Evans as

---

[141] M. Jones, *A Radical Life: The Biography of Megan Lloyd George*, (London, 1991) pp.280-281.

is sometimes suggested, and that Labour was still a strong force in the constituency. However, this could simply be a consequence of the electoral system being sued. Although the by-election had genuine significance in Wales, it could be argued that in the wider context of UK politics, this election is not as significant as it seems.

Overall though, while its importance in the wider context is limited, Carmarthen was significant because despite Labour's dominance, it showed that the Celtic Fringe could be successful in the political machine that is UK politics. Evans' victory in Carmarthen ultimately proved that it was possible for fringe politics to succeed over mainstream parties and this by-election was the first step for formalised Welsh nationalism into Westminster politics.

LINCOLN: 1973
DANIEL BURRILL

The Lincoln by-election of 1973 saw the former Labour Member of Parliament, Dick Taverne, stand against his former party as an Independent Democratic Labour candidate. Taverne resigned his seat as a Labour MP on 6th October 1972, after both the Conservative Party and Labour Party seemed inexorably to be going to the opposite policy extremes, and therefore Taverne decided to take a more moderate approach. This by-election has major significance due to several aspects, the first being by declaring himself an Independent, Taverne highlighted divisions that had existed within the Labour Party itself. It had national significance because this by-election was another example of growing opposition to two-party politics, it represents local support of a national issue, in regards to Europe, and finally due to the fact this by-election, and what Taverne stood for, can arguably be seen as a sign of what was to come for the party, with the creation of the SDP and then when New Labour led the way under Tony Blair.

Dick Taverne 'saw the Labour Party as a lost cause, steadily being taken over by the left, which was not only misguided but would make the party unelectable.'[142] Therefore, Taverne knew that by resigning his position, it would force a by-election to take place. It can be argued that the Labour Party itself during this period was aware it was increasingly moving to the left, as described by Richard Jay; 'In the Spring of 1972, a series of speeches from Jenkins, interpreted by Wilson and his allies as preparing for a bid for the leadership, emphasized the need for Labour to reunite as a party of constructive, radical reform rather than being locked into mere Tory-bashing.'[143] Despite this, Taverne was ahead and therefore 'in one of the most famous by-election campaigns in British history, and with powerful support from both the press and well-known individuals, Taverne won the by-election of 1st March 1973 as a 'Democratic Labour' candidate with a massive 13,000 majority.'[144] With such a majority over the official Labour Party, this by-election is of great significance, and as put by Cook; 'Coming at a time when Liberals and Nationalists were also hammering the established parties, Taverne's triumph

---

[142] N. Stockley, *Dictionary of Liberal Biography*, (Duncan Brack, 1998) p.348
[143] R. Jay, 'Lincoln and the Liberal surge, 1972-73' in *By-elections in British Politics*, (Routledge, 2003) p.197
[144] C. Cook, 'The Challengers to the Two-Party System' in *Trends in British Politics since 1945*, (London, 1978) p.155

seemed yet further evidence of the erosion of the two-party system.'[145] Taverne's success was short lived and he was defeated in October 1974, however, the opposition he showed to the Labour Party makes this by-election important, and as he went on to be a founder of the SDP, it can be seen that this election a long term impact in some respects. Through a series of newspaper articles, this chapter will explore attitudes towards the Lincoln by-election, before, during and after it, and represent the changing views towards this unexpected victory.

On 31st January, 1973, *The Guardian* newspaper published an article entitled 'Taverne affair main issue at Lincoln', which being written a few months before the by-election, is useful in understanding views over who would be likely to win. The article states that the upcoming by-election 'promises to be one of the more piquant events of the 1973 political calendar.'[146] The unusual events of this by-election, having two candidates for Labour, one official and one independent meant that it received press coverage and became an interesting series of events to follow. Standing in the by-election on the right, was Mr Jonathan Guinness who was in support of the Common Market, on the left was Mr John Dilks, who was against the idea of a Common Market, and as reported in the article; 'Between them, or rather hanging over them like some

---

[145] C. Cook, 'The Challengers to the Two-Party System' in *Trends in British Politics since 1945*, (London, 1978) p.155
[146] *The Guardian*, 31st January 1973

sulphurous wizard, is Mr Dick Taverne. He resigned his seat in the Commons in October to fight as an Independent Social Democrat when the Lincoln Labour Party disowned him for voting in favour of membership of the Common Market.'[147] The way Dick Taverne is described as a 'sulphurous wizard', shows how it was not usual that there was someone in that position, and going on to state 'it could have been a good, straightforward fight between Conservatives and Labour in normal times'[148], maybe shows how Taverne's opposition was not looked highly upon. This last statement also is highly relevant in showing how previously two parties were what were expected to run for seats, but Taverne under Democratic Labour now added to the growing opposition to two-party politics across the country. The Liberals won by-elections at Rochdale in 1972 and Sutton and Cheam in the same year, creating a major challenge to the traditional two parties and 'after Sutton, the Liberal bandwagon began to roll, accompanied by a strong Nationalist showing and a sensational personal challenge to the two-party system by Dick Taverne at Lincoln.'[149] The Lincoln by-election of 1973, maybe on its own, cannot be viewed as the greatest challenge, but when put alongside the Liberal resurgence it adds to a significant opposition to the traditional two-party system, and is of great significance due to the personal challenge it created for Labour, showing divisions within the party.

---

[147] *The Guardian*, 31st January 1973
[148] *Ibid.*
[149] C. Cook, 'The Challengers to the Two-Party System' in *Trends in British Politics since 1945*, (London, 1978) p.136

The newspaper article is also of immense value when looking for a contemporary view of why Taverne went alone, containing a quote from himself claiming "One of the things which contributed to my decision to make a stand is that the left wing of the party - it is not true to call it Marxist - the Tribune group, has begun to dominate, indeed has a stranglehold on the party. There is a clear majority on the national executive council of those with whom I disagree."[150] With which the article claims that Taverne thinks 'it is not he who has changed but the Labour Party.'[151]

Just before the by-election, on February 20th, 1973, *The Times* published an article entitled 'Lincoln candidates are busy trying to explain to voters who they are'. This headline makes clear that the unusual circumstances of having two Labour candidates meant that some voters may have been confused as to who they should support. The article reports that 'Mr Dilks, who has fought as a Labour candidate in previous elections, here has to be called "official" Labour Party Candidate - a measure forced on him by the former Labour MP, Mr Taverne.'[152] Here the article, in some respects, does not support Taverne, suggesting he caused a problem by having to change usual voting titles. It is interesting to note that being published just before the by-election, this article did not show any real support for Dick Taverne, and therefore

---

[150] *The Guardian*, 31st January 1973
[151] *Ibid.*
[152] *The Times*, 20th February 1973

could reflect a view that he was not expected to win, especially by the margin he did. The day after the by-election, March 2nd, 1973, *The Guardian* published an article entitled 'Taverne triumphs but Labour holds on at Dundee'. It is useful here to understand how Labour is reported as 'holding on', maybe hinting at the fact a challenge had been created for the two-party system. The article shows the significance of this by-election in a wider context, stating 'Mr Taverne's personal triumph alters the face of British politics overnight. Standing as an Independent Democratic Labour candidate in defiance of the official Labour Party, he crushed not only Labour but also the conservative Party into total insignificance.'[153] Being a national newspaper, and giving this by-election this reported success, shows how it had a major impact on British Politics during this period, creating an independent opposition to a major party, that was supported above and beyond any expectations by the local electorate in Lincoln. The article goes on to state 'nothing quite like it has been seen this century in British elections. Mr Taverne will now become a phenomenon far more extraordinary than the former Mr Eric Lubbock, who stormed to victory over the Conservative Party in the Orpington by-election in 1962.'[154] Comparing this by-election to other significant ones, and in this case giving it higher significance, clearly demonstrates the importance of this by-election, and as Dick Taverne beat the

---

[153] *The Guardian*, 2nd March 1973
[154] *Ibid.*

official Labour candidate John Dilks by 13,191 votes, this was not just a minor win, but a great victory.

It has to be reiterated, that the reason behind Taverne's battle against his own party was because 'in 1971, entry into the Common Market increasingly became the focus of conflict between Labour's Left and Right, the parliamentary leadership and the extra-parliamentary organization.'[155] To cover the left aspect of Labour, Wilson adopted a sceptical position towards the European issue and pro-Europeans, such as Taverne, who were brought to the fore in the late sixties felt isolated and betrayed. Media attention during this period was not focussed on problems within the Conservative government, but those under Labour, and this created a problem over whether the party was properly addressing working class interests. On June 8th, 1973, following on from the by-election, *The Guardian* reported 'Mr Taverne, who resigned from the Labour Party on the EEC issue, and then regained his parliamentary seat at a by-election in March, said : "It's absolutely fantastic. It's certainly the biggest turnaround in local government I've ever known."'[156] Being a few months after the by-election, this *Guardian* article shows how happy Taverne was with the result, but more importantly highlights the reason he went against Labour as an Independent, which was the European issue. Taverne, prior

---

[155] R. Jay, 'Lincoln and the Liberal surge, 1972-73' in *By-elections in British Politics*, (Routledge, 2003) p.196
[156] *The Guardian*, 8th June 1973

to the issue over entry to the Common Market, had problems with Labour however, as Stockley notes; 'At the 1959 conference, Taverne publicly supported Hugh Gaitskell in his unsuccessful attempt to abolish Clause IV of the party constitution.'[157] Clause IV being the section of the Labour Party constitution that supported nationalisation, which for Labour supporters was seen as the most effective way of running the nation's economy. However, it was controversial in that the wording meant it could be interpreted in many ways and it was not reworded until 1995 under Tony Blair. In many respects Taverne's actions, in regards to Clause IV and the European issue, were an early sign of the future of the Labour Party, which was 'New Labour' under Tony Blair, not simply the SDP.

Despite the significant result, and when put alongside other by-elections being seen as major opposition to the two-party system, not everyone saw the Lincoln result as momentous. On June 9th, 1973 *The Guardian* published an article containing a quote from the former Labour Prime Minister 'Mr Harold Wilson [who] described the Lincoln result as a purely local situation with "no significance nationally."'[158] This is a crucial quote in understanding how the official Labour Party responded to the result, and despite being thoroughly beaten by a large margin, maybe to restore confidence in his party, Wilson saw the issue as

---

[157] N. Stockley, *Dictionary of Liberal Biography*, (Duncan Brack, 1998) p.347
[158] *The Guardian*, 9th June 1973

not something that will affect the party in the long run. The fact that such a high profile figure within the Labour Party commented on this by-election though, in many respects highlights its significance as it was being reported on a national level.

During the Lincoln by-election, taking a centre-right approach to Labour, Taverne in many respects was in a centrist position between Labour and Conservative, more or less where the Liberal Party stood at the time. On 8th August, 1974, two months before Taverne lost his Lincoln seat to the official Labour candidate Margaret Jackson (later Margaret Beckett), *The Guardian* produced an article entitled 'Taverne's deal with Liberals?'. The article reported 'If he does decide to leave the Labour benches, where he has sat since his sensational by-election victory in 1973, Mr Taverne will be set for a good deal of trouble in his political base at Lincoln. This is the only part of Britain where his Campaign for Social Democracy has any real significance, following three shattering results in the general election.'[159] It is made clear that as Taverne's campaign for Democratic Labour never reached the success it got at Lincoln in 1973 since, then by moving from Labour to Liberal, he will almost certainly be losing his electorate. The article goes on to state 'The standing defeat of three of his candidates in the last election - none of them reached 1,000 votes even though they were standing

---

[159] *The Guardian*, 8th August 1974

against noted Labour Left-wingers - is said to have convinced Mr Taverne that his one-man attempt to start a Social Democratic movement is doomed. Joining the Liberals however, would involve abandoning his supporters in Lincoln, where the Democratic Labour Party still controls the council.'[160] This newspaper article can be seen as reflecting the demise of Taverne's attempt at Democratic Labour, as by losing votes, and considerations of an alliance with the Liberals meant he could no longer hold on to Labour's core supporters. Despite this, the newspaper does make clear he had not completely lost his support at Lincoln, reporting that 'in the last election he had a majority of only 1,300 over the official Labour candidate, Miss Margaret Jackson, with the Conservative beaten into third place. The majority [however] was only one-tenth the size of the one he gained in his astonishing 1973 by-election victory.'[161] The last newspaper article being addressed contained the heading 'Dick Taverne warns of the perils of putting principle before party', which was published in *The Guardian* on October 10th, 1995. This article is extremely useful in regards to the Lincoln by-election of 1973 and how it fits into a wider context, because here Taverne uses the benefit of hindsight to look back and give advice. Within the article there are a few crucial points made by Taverne, the first being 'What happens when parties change, as they do? Inevitably men and women of independent minds have found themselves out of sympathy with

---

[160] *The Guardian*, 8th August 1974
[161] *Ibid.*

their party's approach. The convention of British Politics nevertheless dictates that they keep their heads down and swallow their consciences.'[162]

Here Taverne is basically talking about himself, in that he saw that the Labour Party had changed and therefore became an independent candidate to stand for what he believed in, but as the following year he failed to hold the seat, he makes clear that British politics in the long run tends not to allow this to happen. Chris Cook argues that 'however unpopular the two major parties may be, in the long term it is they who have survived and their challengers who have been defeated.'[163] This is what happened to Taverne, and in his article in this newspaper he goes on to state that 'in Westminster to betray your principles for the sake of your party is almost a virtue. To stick to your principles and leave your party is an unforgiveable crime.'[164] Here Dick Taverne, with the benefit of hindsight, is able to show how leaving one's party when it changes to become an independent pursuing what a candidate truly believes in, is not made at all easy by the party they leave. This article is extremely useful because it was written by Dick Taverne himself, and as he knows from experience, it shows the challenges and hardship it takes to stand as an independent in trying to oppose one of the two major parties. Without a doubt, the

---

[162] *The Guardian*, 10th October 1995
[163] C. Cook, 'The Challengers to the Two-Party System' in *Trends in British Politics since 1945*, (London, 1978) p.156
[164] *The Guardian*, 10th October 1995

1973 Lincoln by-election had a major significance not just on the local level, but in a wider context too. It represented local opposition to a major party, that contributed to a national growing opposition of two-party politics typified by the Liberal resurgence, and is of immense importance because it shows a candidate standing as an independent and standing against their own party on a matter of policy – in this important case, the UK's membership of the EEC. David Butler claims 'the main interest in by-elections has undoubtedly lain in what they are thought to reveal about the state of public opinion, both in relation to specific issues and to the likely outcome of the next general election.'[165] This by-election expressed opinions concerning the UK's membership of the EEC, and how Labour was split by entry on Heath's Conservative terms. Consequently they changed as a party, resulting in some members, such as Dick Taverne, going back to what they believed were Labour's values. Despite not being a long-term gain, the astonishing result at Lincoln, beating the official Labour candidate and the in-power Conservatives, shows the importance of by-elections in representing local views over national parties. By-elections don't always prove significant, but in regards to opinions on local and national level, 'Independents and minor parties can test whether any groundswell of sympathy exists . . . as Lincoln showed, the possibility is always there.'[166]

---

[165] D. Butler, 'By-elections and their interpretation' in *By-elections in British Politics*, (London, 2003) p.5
[166] *Ibid.*, p.11

FERMANAGH AND SOUTH TYRONE: 1981
RORY TINMAN

The 1981 Fermanagh and South Tyrone by-elections, and the events that surround them, are prominent aspects of the Irish Republican narrative. The winning candidate in the first of these two elections, Republican hunger striker, Bobby Sands remains a controversial and divisive character, not just in Northern Ireland but around the world. Whilst some of his ideological opponents are keen for him to be remembered primarily for his convictions that led to his imprisonment, his supporters work to ensure that he is remembered worldwide as a martyr who played a key role in the Republican struggle. [167][168] Monuments to his efforts for the cause can be found across Ireland and beyond, with streets named after

---

[167] *Belfast Telegraph*, 20th September 2013
[168] *The Daily Mail*, 30th October 2008

him in Tehran and Florence.[169][170] Sands spent sixty-six days on hunger strike in the H-Blocks in Long Kesh prison before his eventual death, during which time he was elected as MP for Fermanagh and South Tyrone with a majority of 1446 votes.[171][172] The ramifications of the campaigns and result of this election were monumental for the criminalisation tactics of the then British government, which largely relied on the claim that prosecuted Republicans had little support, as this chapter will explain. This election result has also been attributed with leading the Republican movement into electoral politics which proved to be a vital development for the decommissioning of the IRA and the wider peace process. This progression of what was considered by many to be a revolutionary fringe movement into mainstream politics will also be examined in this chapter.

The strikes in the H-blocks began as a response to the treatment of Republican prisoners after their political status was revoked in 1976.[173] They began with the 'blanket protest', which involved prisoners refusing to wear prison uniforms and resolving

---

[169] Bobby Sands Trust. 2012. Florence names Bobby Sands St. *Bobby Sands Trust*. [online] Available at: http://www.bobbysandstrust.com/archives/2570 [Date accessed: 15/05.2014]
[170] *Irish Central*, 9th May 2013
[171] D. McKittrick, and D. McVeigh, *Making Sense of the Troubles*. (London, 2001)
[172] T. Hennessy, *Hunger Strike: Margaret Thatcher's Battle with the IRA*. (Kildare, 2014)
[173] D. McKittrick, and D. McVeigh, *Making Sense of the Troubles*. (London, 2001)

to wear nothing but a blanket.[174] This then escalated into the 'dirty protests'. Over the four year duration of these protests prisoners refused to wash and deliberately engaged in severely reducing the hygiene standards of their prison cells.[175] This involved the protesters smearing their faeces on their cell walls and allowing left over food to rot in piles in their cells, amongst other tactics.[176] Richard O'Rawe describes living in these conditions as feeling like 'being buried alive in a sewer'.[177] After these tactics failed to bring about the restoration of political status, the prisoners focussed on intensifying their protests further and began a hunger strike in October 1980.[178] Richard English considers the tactic of hunger striking to be an 'ancient weapon in old Ireland'.[179] It seems only natural that the prisoners came to the decision to engage in such tactics as it was a hunger strike that brought about their original recognition as political prisoners in 1972.[180] The sense of martyrdom associated with this tactic typifies what McBride refers to as the 'pathological fixation [of Irish Republicans] with sacrifice and death'.[181] This 1980 hunger strike ended in confusion as it was called off as one of the strikers neared the point of death in a

---

[174] D. McKittrick, and D. McVeigh, *Making Sense of the Troubles.* (London, 2001)
[175] R. O'Rawe, *Blanketmen* (Dublin, 2005)
[176] *Ibid.*
[177] *Ibid.*
[178] D. McKittrick, and D. McVeigh, *Making Sense of the Troubles.* (London, 2001)
[179] R. English, *Irish freedom: the History of Nationalism in Ireland* (London, 2007)
[180] D. McKittrick, and D. McVeigh, *Making Sense of the Troubles.* (London, 2001)
[181] I. McBride, *History and Memory in Modern Ireland* (Cambridge, 2001)

Belfast hospital. Despite the IRA negotiators claiming a victory, due to some issues with communication between the prisoners' negotiators and their adversaries in the British government, just what concessions were agreed on and how they were to be implemented was left unclear as it eventually transpired that the British government would not meet the demands of the prisoners.[182]

In March the next year the hunger strikes resumed. On this occasion it was agreed that the strikers would fast one by one, with the expectation that in the event of the death of a striker, he was to be replaced by another prisoner in order to be able to keep sustained pressure on the British government over a longer period of time if necessary.[183] Bobby Sands was to be the first of these strikers and began his fast on 1st March.[184] In his diary entry from the first day of his hunger strike Sands wrote '[The hunger strike] has been forced upon me and my comrades by four and a half years of stark inhumanity . . . I am a casualty of a perennial war that is being fought between the oppressed Irish people and an alien, oppressive, unwanted regime that refuses to withdraw from our land'.[185] The demands of the prisoners were as follows:

---

[182] D. McKittrick, and D. McVeigh, *Making Sense of the Troubles.* (London, 2001)
[183] T. Hennessy, *Hunger Strike: Margaret Thatcher's Battle with the IRA.* (Kildare, 2014)
[184] *Ibid.*
[185] B. Sands, *Writings from Prison.* (Lanham, 1997)

1. The right not to wear prison uniform

2. The right not to have to do prison work

3. The right to have free association amongst ourselves

4. The right to receive a weekly parcel, a weekly visit and unlimited letters.

5. The return of all remission lost as a result of the protest.[186]

A statement released by Danny Morrison in his capacity as the Republican press officer read 'We the Republican POWs in the H Blocks of Long Kesh Prison are entitled to and hereby demand political status, and we reject today, as we have consistently rejected every day since September 14th 1976, when the Blanket protest began the British government's attempted criminalisation of ourselves and our struggle'.[187] This release went on to state that 'Only the loud voice of the Irish people and world opinion can bring them to their senses, and only a hunger strike, where lives are laid down as proof of our political convictions, can rally such opinion and present the British with the problem that, far from criminalising the cause of Ireland, their intransigence is actually bringing attention to the cause.'[188] Throughout the protests the British government remained firm on their stance. Soon after the

---

[186] R. O'Rawe, *Blanketmen* (Dublin, 2005)
[187] *Ibid.*
[188] *Ibid.*

beginning of the 1981 hunger strike during a speech in Belfast, Margaret Thatcher stated, "Once again we have a hunger strike at the Maze Prison in the quest for what they call political status. There is no such thing as political murder, political bombing or political violence. There is only criminal murder, criminal bombing and criminal violence. We will not compromise on this. There will be no political status."[189] In her autobiography Thatcher wrote 'All my instincts were against bending to such pressure, and certainly there could be no changes to prison regime once the strike had begun.'[190]

Four days into the strike, the MP for Fermanagh and South Tyrone, Frank Maguire, an independent Nationalist passed away, soon after the writ was moved in parliament for a by-election to select his successor.[191] Given the unprecedented nature of the by-election, putting forward a candidate on behalf of the prisoners was not something that had been considered previously. In an interview with myself carried out as research for this chapter last year, Danny Morrison, the acting spokesperson for the prisoners at the time, claims "nobody was actually thinking of a by-election, we were thinking in terms of the hunger strike publicity".[192] At the Sinn Fein Ard Fheis, annual conference the year before, the national

---

[189] M. Thatcher, *1981 March 5th speech in Belfast*. http://www.margaretthatcher.org/document/104589. [Date Accessed: 10/3/2014]
[190] M. Thatcher, *The Autobiography* (London, 1995)
[191] T. Hennessy, *Hunger Strike: Margaret Thatcher's Battle with the IRA*. (Kildare, 2014)
[192] Danny Morrison, interviewed by Rory Tinman 2013.

executive had rejected a proposal that Sinn Fein should begin contesting elections in the North, on the basis that engaging with political system would mean acknowledging it as legitimate.[193]

Engagement in mainstream politics had traditionally been treated with a considerable degree of scepticism within the Irish republican movement since partition, so the decision to put forward Sands on this occasion was unprecedented not just to the British establishment, but also by large sections of the Republican movement.[194] Morrison recalls the first time he heard of the suggestion, as Jim Gibney, a member of Sin Fein entered the Republican Press Centre and put forward the idea.[195] Although Gibney was the first person Morrison heard the idea from, he later learned that the suggestion had originally been made by Bernadette Devlin McAliskey.[196] Sands was contacted with regard to his potential candidacy. Although he was in favour of the idea, he did not feel that it was going to save him.[197] O'Rawe, who was also interviewed for this chapter recalls the rest of the prisoners also being favourable to the idea as it "would focus the attention on the issue of the prison and on Bobby being on hunger strike."[198] O'Rawe also remembers Sands feeling that his election would not bring about an end to the strike, "In his mind, the chances of him

---

[193] Danny Morrison, interviewed by Rory Tinman 2013.
[194] R. English, *Irish freedom: the History of Nationalism in Ireland* (London, 2007)
[195] Danny Morrison, interviewed by Rory Tinman 2013.
[196] *Ibid.*
[197] *Ibid.*
[198] Richard O'Rawe, interviewed by Rory Tinman. 2014.

surviving the hunger strike were very very small and he did not think within himself that it would be enough to move the British Government to bring about the conditions and a solution."[199] In this sense it seems that Sands had a fairly good impression of the intentions and approach of the British government. Thatcher wrote in her autobiography that 'there was never any question of conceding political status'.[200] From the point of view of O'Rawe and the other prisoners "it was an opportunity and no more. . . There was an opportunity there, it was a strong Nationalist constituency. If they could have had a Nationalist candidate, the seat could be won, it was seen as just an opportunity, a golden opportunity, to highlight the hunger strike."[201] Whilst Morrison and other prominent Republicans were largely in favour of the prospect of Sands running in the election, it was still necessary to have wider support from the movement. A meeting was held across the border in Monaghan to discuss the possibility. Although Morrison was not present at the meeting, he recalls being in contact with Gerry Adams who was in attendance. Adams phoned Morrison to tell him that the motion of putting forward Sands for election had been rejected.[202] There were simply too many uncertainties surrounding the prospect of Sands candidacy as Morrison discussed; "What if the vote was split? What if the SDLP stood? What if he lost? The effects it would have on morale etc.

---

[199] Richard O'Rawe, interviewed by Rory Tinman. 2014.
[200] M. Thatcher, *The Autobiography* (London, 1995)
[201] Richard O'Rawe, interviewed by Rory Tinman. 2014.
[202] Danny Morrison, interviewed by Rory Tinman 2013.

and on the campaign itself."[203] However, there were some members that arrived late to the meeting in Monaghan as they had been held up crossing the border by the Ulster Defence Regiment (UDR) and the British Army. The poll was taken on Sands' candidacy once these members arrived and it transpired that Sands had the support of the voting members.[204]

Although Republican support for Sands' candidacy had been made clear, there was still a great degree of uncertainty surrounding his campaign. Sands was only to stand on the condition that there would be no other Nationalist candidates, as he would be facing one Unionist candidate; Harry West of the UUP.[205] Noel Maguire, the brother of the previous MP for the constituency was considering standing, and had a considerable amount of support from Nationalist members of the electorate but eventually withdrew under what Morrison describes as 'tremendous emotional pressure'.[206] However, there was still the question as to whether the SDLP would field a candidate and risk splitting the Nationalist vote. They eventually absented themselves from the election over fears of a backlash as they could have been accused of being responsible for splitting the Nationalist vote and handing Harry West a victory in what was essentially perceived to

---

[203] Danny Morrison, interviewed by Rory Tinman 2013.
[204] *Ibid.*
[205] T. Hennessy, *Hunger Strike: Margaret Thatcher's Battle with the IRA.* (Kildare, 2014)
[206] D. Morrison, *Thirty three thousand, four hundred and ninety two: On the Election of Bobby Sands*, 2001 *Anderstown News.*

be a Nationalist constituency.[207][208] So Sands would be given a clear run at the Nationalist vote, however, there was still a great deal of work to be done on convincing typically non-violent Catholics to vote for a convicted member of the IRA and both the Republican movement and the British government were well aware of this as they worked on their propaganda campaigns.

At the time of the campaign, Republican newspaper *An Phoblacht* predicted that Bobby Sands would become a household name off the back of his strike and election campaign.[209] In his book *Blanketmen*, O'Rawe recalls opponents of Sands, including Harry West using the phrase "A vote for Bobby Sands is a vote for the IRA".[210] This demonstrates how the campaign against Sands aimed to target Nationalist voters who would typically not have supported the armed struggle. Humphrey Atkins, the Secretary of State for Northern Ireland at the time, reportedly believed that the best weapons to fight Sands with were Harry West and the non-violent Catholic population.[211] In consciously aiming to play on Sands' convictions and IRA membership, the campaign against Bobby Sands can be viewed as a further extension of criminalisation tactics. The photograph of Sands that circulated

---

[207] D. Morrison, *Thirty three thousand, four hundred and ninety two: On the Election of Bobby Sands*, 2001 *Anderstown News*.
[208] T. Hennessy, *Hunger Strike: Margaret Thatcher's Battle with the IRA*. (Kildare, 2014)
[209] *Ibid.*
[210] Richard O'Rawe interviewed by Rory Tinman. 2014.
[211] T. Hennessy, *Hunger Strike: Margaret Thatcher's Battle with the IRA*. (Kildare, 2014)

round the media at the time has now become the most recognisable picture of him. Morrison describes it as a "very romantic, pacifist image". Morrison recalls the Northern Ireland Office's (NIO) attempts to replace this as the dominant image with one taken upon his arrest holding a prison number under his chin, effectively being portrayed as a criminal. However, it was too late and the photo of him now replicated on a mural on the Falls Road remained the established image[212]. Meanwhile, Neil Blaney, a somewhat outspoken Southern Fianna Fail politician claimed that a voter for Sands was actually a vote against the institutional violence of the British government and prison services.[213]

Sands' camp's campaign focused far more on the personal appeal rather than the Republican appeal of the election (Hennessy). This is exemplified by the decision to run on an 'Anti-H-blocks' ticket as opposed to a Sinn Fein one. The emotional and personal aspects of the campaign may explain why the British government were unsuccessful. In Margaret Thatcher's biography, *Not for Turning*, Charles Moore notes that she found the Irish preference for cultural politics to be irritating.[214] The emotional aspect of the campaign worked well to engage non-violent Catholic voters. Morrison claims that "the fact that seven men were on hunger strike in 1980 started to bring out middle class people,

---

[212] Danny Morrison, interviewed by Rory Tinman. 2013.
[213] T. Hennessy, *Hunger Strike: Margaret Thatcher's Battle with the IRA*. (Kildare, 2014)
[214] C. Moore *Margaret Thatcher: the Authorised Biography. Volume 1, Not for Turning.* (London, 2013)

teachers, you know civil servants, lawyers, business people . . . So it was obvious that the hunger strike and the prison situation had touched a rare nerve".[215] Richard English also notes that many of the people who voted for Sands 'did not support his or his comrades' violence'.[216] They sided with him and the prisoners in their demands to be treated as political rather than criminal actors. In this sense it could be argued that the support shown by many of the voters was not for the violent agenda associated with Republicanism, but was a call for a renewed approach to the concerns of Irish nationalists and an end to the myopically intransigent tactics of the British government. In claiming that 'a vote for Bobby Sands is a vote for the IRA' it could be said that opponents of Republicanism shot themselves in the foot as they allowed for the impression to be given that the IRA had a mandate off the back of Sands' election victory, rather than only demonstrating a mandate for the strike. Morrison claims that in many Republican areas "we by and large did not vote, we did not see the value in it, because votes were meaningless. They did not produce results."[217] Despite this, there was a great deal of mobilisation for the election in the face of what Morrison considers to be deliberate attempts to hamper the campaign. Morrison claims that "there was a lot of harassment, we were stopped regularly at check points and held for half an hour or an hour, just to slow

---

[215] Danny Morrison, interviewed by Rory Tinman. 2013
[216] R. English, *Irish freedom: the History of Nationalism in Ireland* (London, 2007)
[217] *Ibid.*

down our canvassing efforts."[218]

The Northern Ireland Office (NIO) refused permission for a number of Republicans involved in the campaign to access Bobby Sands in prison, however, Owen Carron who acted as Sands' election agent on the outside was granted access.[219] Carron requested that journalists be allowed access to interview Sands for the purpose of the election, after all, it seemed appropriate that the public should be allowed to get an impression of the man who they might potentially vote for but the denied this request. Carron argued that Sands was a valid candidate and was being denied his rights as such. Furthermore, Sands' camp claimed that the limitations imposed on Sands by the NIO were in contravention of the Representation of the Peoples Act.[220] In a statement from Sands, dictated to Carron he claimed, 'I am being denied my rights as a valid candidate. This typifies the NIO attempts to play down what is happening in the H-blocks.'[221] O'Rawe described the prison at the time as being like a "propaganda factory". Of course, given their limited access to the electorate, the prisons did not resemble a typical campaign headquarters. O'Rawe discussed with me some of the tactics he and other prisoners had to employ to communicate with the campaign outside the prison:

---

[218] R. English, *Irish freedom: the History of Nationalism in Ireland* (London, 2007)
[219] T. Hennessy, *Hunger Strike: Margaret Thatcher's Battle with the IRA.* (Kildare, 2014)
[220] *Ibid.*
[221] *Ibid.*

"If I was doing a letter, I just wrote it on cigarette papers in very very small writing, completely small. I rolled it up into almost a wee quarter inch square communication, put stretch and seal in it, and smuggled it out up your nose and then when you were walking round, pretended to sneeze and put the com into your mouth. Other guys used to smuggle coms out under their foreskin. There was always a genius way of doing it but you always got the coms out."

In a Northern Ireland Office internal communication it was noted that 'many must regard the election as make-or-break . . . If Sands loses badly it is difficult to see how the campaign could continue with any credibility'.[222] This shows the risk incurred on the part of the Republicans that was potentially playing on their minds on the day of the results. Morrison recalls how it was widely assumed by people who "hadn't done their homework" that Sands could not win.[223] Morrison could justly include the NIO among these people who "hadn't done their homework" as they noted that 'the result surprised most observers who had expected a larger proportion of Catholic voters to abstain or spoil their votes rather than vote for a convicted terrorist'.[224] With a turnout of 86.7% of the vote, Bobby Sands won 30,492 votes to Harry West's 29,046

---

[222] T. Hennessy, *Hunger Strike: Margaret Thatcher's Battle with the IRA.* (Kildare, 2014)
[223] Danny Morrison, interviewed by Rory Tinman. 2013
[224] T. Hennessy, *Hunger Strike: Margaret Thatcher's Battle with the IRA.* (Kildare, 2014)

giving him a majority of 1446 votes.[225] Richard O'Rawe recalls hearing of the news inside the prison,

"We had these pocket, wee miniature crystal, radios which we hid up our arses and he [Brendan 'Bik' McFarlane] had the radio out so he was listening to the result and he put the radio away and shouted down to me. "Win Bobby, Bobby won". The whole wing heard it. Then he shouted down "look nobody, don't let the screws know that we know". . . It was greeted with absolute elation in the H-blocks. . . I tell you it was one of the best feelings that I ever had in my life. Since I heard the news, I nearly cried, I feel like crying now, I swear, it was fantastic."

Despite the clear emotion felt by the prisoners, they must have been successful in masking their elation as prison authorities claimed that Sands' victory produced little response in the prison.[226] Morrison recollects the events after the announcement of the result, "When Harry West got up to speak he took a piece of paper out of his pocket and he began reading it and it was his victory speech. He had only written one speech because he couldn't believe that Bobby Sands was going to get elected".[227] Bobby Sands' agent Owen Carron had also prepared a victory speech in which he stated, "The voters of Fermanagh and South

---

[225] D. McKittrick, and D. McVeigh, *Making Sense of the Troubles.* (London, 2001)
[226] T. Hennessy, *Hunger Strike: Margaret Thatcher's Battle with the IRA.* (Kildare, 2014)
[227] Danny Morrison, interviewed by Rory Tinman. 2013

Tyrone stood by the prisoners and told Mrs Thatcher today that we, on behalf of the Irish people, will not accept the situation in the H-Blocks and we demand an immediate end to the intolerable situation." This shows how the Republican camp clearly saw the victory as a blow to the British government's criminalisation tactics.

Whilst this may have been the view of the Republicans, the British government seemed determined not to have their tactics undermined. Thatcher asked Sir Michael Havers, Attorney General at the time, to provide a legal opinion on the law in relation to parliamentary candidates serving a prison sentence. He informed her that Sands was not disqualified from taking his seat, although he of course would not be able to attend parliament, due to his incarceration.[228] The proposal of expelling him from the House as unfit for membership was considered and Parliament was urged to do so by *The Times* newspaper however, expulsion would not prevent him from standing again and causing further embarrassment.[229][230] Sands released a statement to the press in the aftermath of his election addressing the prospect of his expulsion stating that if he was expelled 'Ireland and the rest of the world will continue to recognize the democratic decision of the people even if the British Parliament cannot abide by the very tenets

---

[228] Danny Morrison, interviewed by Rory Tinman. 2013
[229] *Ibid.*
[230] *United Press International*, 11th April 1981

which it professes to uphold'.[231] So it was apparent that expulsion was a strategy that could potentially backfire on the British government. It was decided soon after Sands' election that the Representation of the People Act would be changed subsequently to prevent any further prisoners standing.[232] This meant that after Sands' death after 66 days on hunger strike and 26 days into his term as an MP, his agent Owen Carron would have to stand for the next by election, as opposed to running another striker as O'Rawe suggests would have been a possibility. Carron went on to win and only increased the share of the vote for the Anti-H-blocks movement.[233] Sands' death prompted widespread reactions including several days of rioting in parts of Northern Ireland.[234] In Prime Minister's Questions after Sands' death Thatcher responded to a question which accused her of allowing Sands' death through intransigence regarding the hunger strikers, replying, "Mr. Sands was a convicted criminal. He chose to take his own life. It was a choice that his organisation did not allow to many of its victims".[235] Despite the outrage that met Sands' success in Britain, it is estimated that somewhere in the region of 100,000 people attended his funeral.[236]

The response to the hunger strikes and Bobby Sands'

---

[231] *Associated Press*, April 12th 1981
[232] Representation of the People Act 1981, *UK Parliament*
[233] D. McKittrick, and D. McVeigh, *Making Sense of the Troubles*. (London, 2001)
[234] CAIN, Chronology of the Conflict – 1981, 2013
[235] Thatcher, M. 1981 March 5th House of Commons PQs
[236] CAIN, Chronology of the Conflict – 1981, 2013

election had considerable consequences for the British government's criminalisation strategy, as it was intended to. O'Rawe claims that the whole purpose of the election was mainly to undermine the British establishment who claimed that there was no support for the hunger strike. He went on to claim that the election result made it "impossible to ignore us . . . It was no longer possible for the British Government to keep this down in the 4th division, it had moved from 4th division to premier league overnight".[237] Dawson claims that Sands' victory entirely went against the British government's and large sections of the media's assertion that the IRA were a plague of rebels with no support.[238] However, this can mostly be put down to the propaganda efforts of the British government during the campaign claiming that support for Sands equated to support for the IRA. It might be more appropriate to view the support for Sands as more of an anti-British vote, than a pro-IRA vote. It is of great importance that Sands ran on an Anti-H-block ticket, yet this was largely ignored from the British perspective, which seemed to be so caught up in the lens of criminalisation rather than the possibility of prisoners and Republican supporters having legitimate concerns which were not appropriately taken into consideration. This is exemplified in Margaret Thatcher's autobiography in which she refers to the special category status afforded to prisoners in 1972 as a 'bad

---

[237] Richard O'Rawe interviewed by Rory Tinman. 2014.
[238] G. Dawson, *Making Peace with the Past: Memory, Trauma and the Irish Troubles*. (Manchester, 2007)

mistake'.[239] Seldon and Collings write that 'Mrs Thatcher was resolute in her attitude that the strikers were common criminals and there would be absolutely no question of concessions'.[240] This shows how the shadow of criminalisation was cast over the proceedings of the strike and election and conditioned British opinion such that the British government were unprepared to have their stance challenged.[241]

Moore notes that Republicans thought that if Sands was elected to parliament the case for political status would be unquestionable.[242] Criminalisation aimed to delegitimise the political motivations of prisoners, yet here was a Republican prisoner had just won a significant political victory, not just over his opponent Harry West, but also over Thatcher and her government.[243] The strategy of criminalisation meant that it was easy for the British government to ignore the concerns of Republicans. Danny Morrison recalls the approach of Margaret Thatcher saying, "Mrs Thatcher had, I think, the previous year when people had asked her to intervene, turned round and said "how can I talk to them, sure they don't have a mandate" and now Bobby Sands was elected, had a mandate and still she would not

---

[239] M. Thatcher, *The Autobiography.* (London, 1995)
[240] A. Seldon, and D. Collings, *Britain Under Thatcher* (London, 2000)
[241] D. Moen, 'Irish Political Prisoners and Post Hunger-Strike Resistance to Criminalisation.' *British Society of Criminology.* Vol. 3. (1999)
[242] C. Moore *Margaret Thatcher: the Authorised Biography. Volume 1, Not for Turning.* (London, 2013)
[243] D. Moen, 'Irish Political Prisoners and Post Hunger-Strike Resistance to Criminalisation.' *British Society of Criminology.* Vol. 3. (1999)

talk".[244] O'Rawe, in his interview expressed similar sentiments claiming that by still refusing to negotiate with Republicans and address the prison issues the British government had devalued their own democratic process, saying, "the British Government's attitude to democracy is that it is fantastic providing it works for them. If it doesn't work for them, as we have seen from Fermanagh/South Tyrone, they change the rules and they start excluding those who are their political opponents".[245] In this sense, by continuing with criminalisation tactics, the British government failed to delegitimise the IRA but actually delegitimised their own tactics by clinging to them in face of a convincing mandate for Sands and his cause. Richard English notes that the tactics of the British government with regards to the hunger strikes provoked rage in the Nationalist community and potentially 'generated much energy for the Provisional movement to use in coming years', meaning that the prolonging of criminalisation was counter-productive to the efforts of opponents of Republicanism.[246]

Both Bobby Sands and then Owen Carron's successes in the two 1981 Fermanagh and South Tyrone by-elections had a profound effect on the Republican movement. As mentioned before, mainstream politics had traditionally been treated with an air of scepticism by many Republicans. Morrison claims that "in the Republican psyche often is the fear that politics equals

---

[244] Danny Morrison, interviewed by Rory Tinman. 2013
[245] Richard O'Rawe, interviewed by Rory Tinman. 2014.
[246] R. English, *Irish freedom: the History of Nationalism in Ireland* (London, 2007)

constitutionalism equals compromise".[247] This hostility towards electoral politics can be traced back to 1926, when Fianna Fail broke away from Sinn Fein to contest elections in Leinster House.[248] Richard English notes that there was 'something inevitable – or even foreseen and intended – about the development from hunger strike election success in 1981 to the 1990s peace process and to the IRA's eventual cessation of its military campaign'.[249] Indeed, in an article for the *Anderstown News* Danny Morrison claims that the election results of Sands and Carron 'provided the springboard for the electoral rise of Sinn Fein'.[250]

Although Thatcher considered the outcome of the strikes to be a considerable defeat for the IRA, it could be said that the successful foray into electoral politics off the back of the strikes represented the beginning of a successful period for Republicanism. This transition into electoral politics was initially characterised by Danny Morrison's notorious "Armalite in one hand and a ballot paper in the other" quote.[251] This shows how the electoral side of the Republican movement was initially only intended as complementary to the armed strategy. In fact, Sinn Fein was previously considered by many to be subordinate to the IRA and as 'little more than a political mask or mouthpiece for the

---

[247] Danny Morrison, interviewed by Rory Tinman. 2013
[248] R. English, *Irish freedom: the History of Nationalism in Ireland* (London, 2007)
[249] *Ibid.*
[250] Morrison, D. 2001. Thirty three thousand, four hundred and ninety two: On the Election of Bobby Sands. *Anderstown News.*
[251] P. Taylor, *Beyond the Mask: The IRA and Sinn Fein.* (New York, 1997)

group'.[252]

However, Sands and Carron's wins showed that electoral success could be used to prove support for the movement in a way that the armed struggle could not. The armed struggle could be easily dismissed by the British government, allowing for their criminalisation tactics to prevail as the dominant lens through which the movement and its concerns were viewed. Elections showing support for the movement, on the other hand, could work to legitimise the concerns of Republicans, as well as the movement itself.

Ian McAllister notes that in 1981, two Sinn Fein ministers in a power sharing government in 1998 would have been unthinkable let alone the four positions they hold now, including Deputy First Minister.[253][254] At the Sinn Fein Ard Fheis in 1982 it was proposed that if a Northern Ireland Assembly was to go ahead, as suggested by the new secretary of state, Jim Prior, that Sinn Fein would contest seats. The vote on this proposal was nearly lost as many members were under the impression that the elections of Sands and Carron was just a one off intervention for the sake of the hunger strikes, which had now ended.[255] It was at this meeting that Morrison coined the phrase "armalite in one hand and a ballot

---

[252] R. English, *Irish freedom: the History of Nationalism in Ireland* (London, 2007)
[253] I. McAllister, '"The Armalite and the ballot box": Sinn Fein's electoral strategy in Northern Ireland.' *Electoral Studies,* 23 (2004) pp.123-142
[254] Northern Ireland Executive. *Ministers and their Departments*, 2014
[255] Danny Morrison, interviewed by Rory Tinman. 2013.

paper in the other", which he claims was totally unplanned.[256]

Recalling this meeting Morrison claims that, "In a sense, I was playing to the gallery. Of course, I wanted to win over militants who felt that, you know, this would lead to the end of the IRA. I was trying to assure him no, it was quite possible for a movement to be fighting elections and at the same time for the IRA to wage its campaign. So we won the vote and it was that year, 1981, became the springboard for the whole electoral strategy." Morrison attributes the public support generated by the hunger strikes and Sands' and Carron's elections with Sinn Fein participating in the 1982 Northern Ireland Assembly elections, in which the party won 10.1% of the first preference votes, despite only standing in 12 constituencies.[257] This rose to 13.4% of the vote at the Westminster elections the following year. O'Brien described these successes as 'the stuff of political earthquakes'.[258] This direction of the Republican movement came to be accepted as a success by many. In 1986 Gerry Adams made the claim, "there is now a realisation in Republican circles that armed struggle on its own is inadequate and that non-armed forms of political struggle are at least as important".[259]

Despite the electoral success of Sinn Fein, the direction of

---

[256] Danny Morrison, interviewed by Rory Tinman. 2013.
[257] I. McAllister, '"The Armalite and the ballot box": Sinn Fein's electoral strategy in Northern Ireland.' *Electoral Studies,* 23 (2004) pp.123-142
[258] B. O'Brien, 1999. *The Long War: The IRA and Sinn Fein* (New York, 1999)
[259] I. McAllister, '"The Armalite and the ballot box": Sinn Fein's electoral strategy in Northern Ireland.' *Electoral Studies,* 23 (2004) pp.123-142

the Republican movement was not welcomed by all. In interview, I asked Morrison whether in spite of the move into electoral politics Republicanism can still carry on a movement all about resistance and fighting oppression. He admitted that it could not still be viewed as such a movement, but was adamant that Sinn Fein was still different from other parties saying, "I think that Sinn Fein as an anti-imperialist organisation, you know, I think it has established its credentials, it is distinguished from other political parties because of its past. I mean one other party leader was in jail, Martin McGuinness, Deputy First Minster was in jail, Gerry Adams was in jail, Pat Sheehan who's an MLA was in jail, Caral Ni Chullin who's the Cultural Minister was in jail, Raymond McCartney who's an MLA was in jail".[260] Richard English claims that at the time of Sands' candidacy the Republican leadership could have had no way of telling that Republicanism would be able to move in this direction.[261] Richard O'Rawe on the other hand believes that the movement into electoral politics may have been the intention of some of those higher up in the organisation from the outset, he claims that,

"4 of them [the Army Council] were very very set in their way in that they were convinced that armed struggle was the way forward and they thought at that time it was a dawning or a realisation on the Adams faction that armed struggle wasn't the

---

[260] Danny Morrison, interviewed by Rory Tinman. 2013.
[261] R. English, *Irish freedom: the History of Nationalism in Ireland* (London, 2007)

way forward and that this was an opportunity for them to get involved in electoral politics that whetted their appetite and which led eventually to them having their way: the arms struggle being set aside in favour of constitutional politics."[262]

O'Rawe believes that "the Republican movement is not a very revolutionary organisation now".[263] Whilst O'Rawe considers the 1981 elections as still being part of what was a revolutionary movement, he considers the movement towards almost complete engagement with electoral politics to be somewhat of a betrayal of the prisoners, saying "Bobby Sands did not die for Sinn Fein to become a parliamentary party taking seats in Stormont. Bobby Sands died for socialist republic".[264] The outlook of the prisoners, according to O'Rawe was that the hunger strike "was part of a newer revolutionary struggle that would in itself act as a catalyst for the armed struggle of the IRA".[265] O'Rawe believes that Sinn Fein have adopted a position whereby the ends justify the means and that the political success of the party is prioritised.[266] In hindsight, taking into consideration the further electoral gains made off the back of the Sands' success it could be said that the hunger strike indirectly worked as a catalyst against the armed struggle as it paved the way for the transition into electoral politics for the Republican movement.

---

[262] Richard O'Rawe, interviewed by Rory Tinman. 2014.
[263] *Ibid.*
[264] *Ibid.*
[265] *Ibid.*
[266] *Ibid.*

It is likely that had the Republican movement not taken up electoral politics the peace process would have taken a lot longer than it has. After all, having a strong political wing of the movement ultimately allowed for decommissioning to take place. It is also hard to fathom all of the main political parties in Northern Ireland engaging in peace talks with Sinn Fein whilst there was still an active armed movement affiliated with the party. In this sense, Bobby Sands' election can be viewed as inadvertently signposting the Republican movement towards a position that allowed Sinn Fein to play an essential and pivotal role in the peace process. Had Sands not won the election it is likely that Sinn Fein would not have proceeded with engaging in electoral politics, at least not for some time. Whilst the British government, were not to know it at the time, if their propaganda efforts had been successful in deterring constituents from voting for Sands, it is possible that the peace process could have been delayed by years, if not decades. The support demonstrated for Sands hugely undermined the British government's agenda of criminalisation. Their decision to prevent criminals from standing in the future clearly did not prevent further embarrassment nor did it contribute to any success for criminalisation, as Carron's election no doubt caused further embarrassment for Thatcher and her administration. It comes as no surprise that the election results get little mention in Margaret Thatcher's autobiography.[267] The fact that Sands and his fellow hunger strikers were allowed to die despite the election success

---

[267] M. Thatcher, *The Autobiography.* (London, 1995)

only provided further fuel for ill-will towards the British government amongst large sections of the Nationalist community.

This ill-will has lasted decades after the events of 1981 as parties celebrating Thatcher's death were rife in West Belfast and Derry in 2013, thirty-two years later.[268] Whilst the peace process can be partially attributed to Sinn Fein's engagement with electoral politics, sparked by Sands and Carron's success, the result did little for inter-communal relations in Fermanagh and South Tyrone or for that matter across Northern Ireland. Current MLA for the constituency, Arlene Foster of the Democratic Unionist Party, notes that the result led to a sense of distrust of Catholics within the Unionist community.[269] Although the eventual peace in the province can indirectly and partially be attributed to this by-election, this was never the intention of Sands and the other prisoners, and it is highly unlikely that those higher up in the movement had as much foresight as to be able to predict the wider consequences decades after their successful campaign.

---

[268] *The Guardian*, 9th April
[269] G. Dawson, *Making Peace with the Past: Memory, Trauma and the Irish Troubles*. (Manchester, 2007)

MITCHAM AND MORDEN: 1982
BEN MANLEY

The election of Angela Rumbold as MP for Mitcham and Morden on June 2nd 1982 may, on initial reflection, signify a victory for a candidate that reflected the national popularity of the party she represented. Nonetheless, the reasons for such popularity at a local level, the relative unpopularity of the SDP and Labour Party both locally and nationally, added to public attitudes towards them both at the national level. Local, national and international factors should all be taken into consideration when evaluating the significance of this particular contest. In a *Times* column the day after voting, Julian Haviland questions the extent to which both the popularity of the Conservative Party, led by Prime Minister Margaret Thatcher, and the unpopularity of Argentinian President

Galtieri played in the outcome of the result.[270] What the columnist fails to take into account however, when assessing the reasoning behind his prediction of the outcome of the result, are the alternative national or local issues that could have been equally significant factors in the Conservative victory. This chapter will analyse the issues that caused the overturning of Labour holding this seat, before assessing the significance the election had on the Thatcher administration, the Conservative Party and the Liberal/SDP Alliance in the wider context of its spectacular series of election successes between 1981 and 1983.

The political environment in which the by-election took place was at a time when the UK was in the process of confronting both an international military conflict and major domestic challenges. The Royal Marines had advanced to within twenty-five miles of Port Stanley in their objective to recapture the Falkland Islands by the 30th of May 1982.[271] Positive public opinion towards the government had increased as the conflict proceeded and by the 26th of May in a national poll of 400 people for *The Economist* revealed 51% of those surveyed stated they would vote Conservative if an election was held the following day.[272] Furthermore, the SDP candidate Bruce Douglas-Mann claimed that the press coverage of the conflict was an unnecessary distraction

---

[270] *The Times*, 3rd June 1982
[271] *The Telegraph*, 2nd April 2012
[272] The Falklands War - Panel Survey, Published June 1982, Fieldwork 14 April - 23 June 1982, IPSOS Mori

away from his newly created party – the SDP.[273] Therefore, the Falklands conflict did not only affect the national political outlook but the very focus on the conflict by the press, at this stage reporting the increasingly positive news from the islands. This focus on national, arguably international issues, rather overshadowed what would have otherwise been key political local issues. Douglas-Mann may have had a case in his claim that the Falklands War enabled the Conservatives to persuade those who would otherwise have voted for Labour or the SDP thanks to the nationalistic, patriotic fervour of the time. In a national Gallup/Daily Telegraph poll of the 12th April 1982, with the conflict just under way, the Conservatives trailed the SDP by 5.5%.[274] At this early stage in the conflict, aircraft carriers HMS Hermes and HMS Invincible which had set sail from Portsmouth as part of a task force of more than 120 ships were still 2 weeks away from arriving at the Falklands and Lord Carrington had recently resigned as Foreign Secretary. This consequently reinforces the point that the war played a substantial role in the undermining of the electoral chances of Douglas-Mann and the Labour candidate David Nicholas.

Alternatively, it could be conceived that even before the start of the Falklands War, Angela Rumbold, the Conservative candidate, would have been elected as MP for Mitcham and Morden irrespective of whether the Falklands War had taken place

---

[273] *The Times*, 2nd June 1982
[274] 1979- 1983 Polls, Gallup/Telegraph Poll 12th April 1982

or not. In a National Poll taken by the Daily Mail/NOP on 5th February 1982, 2 months before the conflict began, the Conservatives held a 5% lead over Labour who came in second.[275] Additionally, the conflict may also have proven irrelevant due to the fact that Douglas-Mann came third in the 1983 General Election in the same constituency with a 2% drop in the vote while the Labour candidate Nicholas gained 4.4% of the vote.[276] Thus, this result not only shows the beneficial impact the SDP split from the Labour Party had for the Conservatives in Mitcham and Morden, surpassing the importance of the Falklands Conflict, but additionally, Douglas-Mann had been elected as an MP largely due to his membership of the Labour Party, as opposed to the constituents granting him the seat thanks to his competency as a local MP and ignoring his switch of allegiance.

Without question the ongoing battle for the Falklands assisted the Conservatives in this by-election, although the decision by Bruce Douglas-Mann to change allegiance to the SDP and going against the norm, by making his personal decision to resign his seat and call a by-election, has to be one of the key explanations as to why Labour and the SDP gave themselves minimal chances of success in the contest. The SDP had split from Labour in 1981 and later that year agreed an alliance with the Liberal Party.[277] Furthermore, the SDP were competing in another

---

[275] 1979- 1983 Polls, NOP/Daily Mail Poll 5th February 1982,
[276] *The Times*, 4th June 1983
[277] *BBC News*, 25th January 2001

key marginal by-election - Glasgow Hillhead - in March 1982 and the party leadership was reluctant for Douglas-Mann to announce the need for a by-election causing the party to split attention and resources away from Roy Jenkins own contest.[278] On the other hand, Rumbold outflanked both Labour and the SDP being "an active exponent of the Conservative right" according to *The Guardian*, thereby allowing her to appeal to the working class constituents.[279] Furthermore, Rumbold, having served on the nearby Richmond Council for 9 years, would have appealed to the electorate more or less to the same degree as Douglas-Mann in his claim of being a 'local' candidate. Consequently, had Douglas-Mann remained as a representative of the Labour Party, or even if either Labour or an SDP candidate had competed for the seat, Rumbold may well have been defeated, or at least her margin of victory would have been reduced significantly, the centre-left was split as it would be at the following general election.

In the build-up to the contest the Mitcham and Morden constituency was described in *The Times* as a "highly marginal seat."[280] The reasoning for such constantly closely fought contests was predominantly down to the social composition of the constituency, including specific factors seen at the 1982 by-election. For example, the number of people employed in outer London boroughs in 1981, of which Mitcham and Morden is part,

---

[278] *The Glasgow Herald*, 21st January 1982
[279] *The Guardian*, 4th September
[280] *The Times*, 20th January 1982

peaked in 1981 and was in steady decline until 1996.[281] On the other hand, demographic statistics also demonstrate that there was depopulation in Mitcham, Merton and Morden between 1971- 1981 with a fall of 5214 in that period.[282] With such paradoxical figures it could be argued that the Mitcham and Morden constituency, with such a divergent socio-economic composition, could result in potentially tightly fought contests. The class make-up of the constituency can be linked to the importance of Douglas-Mann essentially splitting the working class vote. Although hypothetical, had the SDP and Labour had a combined vote in the election they would have accumulated a combined vote of 16,507; 3201 more than Rumbold. However, it should also be noted that the Conservative swing from Labour was 10.2% in the election, demonstrating that there was a reduction in partisan alignment in this election from certain elements of the working class in the constituency drawn to Rumbolds' populist, working class conservatism.[283] For example, *The Independent* later described her as a "staunch Thatcherite and monarchist" with a "strong interest in education."[284] Furthermore, the fact that a proportion of previously Labour voters had voted Conservative dismisses the notion that had either Labour or the SDP not competed for the seat, a Conservative defeat would have been inevitable.

---

[281] I. Turok, and N. Edge, 'The jobs gap in Britain's cities: Employment loss and labour market consequences', *The Policy Press* (1999) p.62
[282] 1801 - 1981 Census figures, Merton Council
[283] *The Times*, 4th June 1982
[284] *The Independent*, 23rd June 2010

At a national level, the SDP/Liberal Alliance, by the end of 1981, had amassed considerable support. Yet, political commentators began to question whether this short lived honeymoon period had come to an abrupt halt. Hugh Stephenson argues that "by March 1982, the SDP leaders were saying privately that they thought their party was sufficiently well established to be able to survive some single disaster."[285]

The signs for a politically difficult time ahead were forecast in a *Times* article in January 1982 however. Issues on policies, financing and the nature of the Alliance itself all had the potential to cause ruptures in the coalition's cohesiveness.[286] The article also postulates that "the evidence of by-election results and opinion polls that voters are more positively attracted by the Alliance itself rather than by either of its two components, ought to be pushing the two parties closer together."[287] This evidence is reinforced by John Stevenson, who opines "it was significant that the peak of Alliance support had already been passed when the fortunes of all parties, but especially the Conservatives, became bound up with the extraneous event of the Falkland Conflict."[288] Consequently, for Douglas-Mann to lose significant support of the SDP leadership, "who regarded his decision [to cause a by-election] as an act of political self-indulgence" and thus present the Alliance as a divided

---

[285] H. Stephenson, *Claret and Chips, The Rise of the SDP* (London, 1982) p.168
[286] *The Times*, 4th January 1982
[287] *Ibid.*
[288] J. Stevenson, *Third Party Politics since 1945, Liberals, Alliance and Liberal Democrats*, (London, 1993) p.80

group, it cannot be discounted in playing a significant part in his electoral defeat.[289]

Nationally, the Conservative Party on the other hand, having endured a stormy couple of years in office since their 1979 electoral victory, were by 1982, making a slow and gradual recovery with an upturn in the economy, reflecting itself in opinion polls. Before early spring of 1982, however, the national economic situation was still volatile with a Conservative Party that had the potential to become as divided and unstable as the Labour Party of the time. In an article in *The Washington Post* in October 1981, "Edward Heath and a number of other critics urged Thatcher's government to try alternative policies to reduce record unemployment, avert more business failures and lift Britain out of its worst recession in half a century."[290] However, the financial and unemployment crisis appeared to be ending just before the start of the Falklands conflict. In the second economic quarter of 1982, the UK's GDP grew by 1.3%, alongside increased consumer expenditure during this time with £35,750 million spent in the second half of 1981, increasing to £36,000 million spent in the first half of 1982. Therefore, the government's gradual improvement of the national economy could well have had an impact in the Mitcham and Morden by-election. However, as the South- East of

---

[289] H. Stephenson, *Claret and Chips, The Rise of the SDP* (London, 1982) p.168
[290] Thatcher Policy Splits Ranks of Conservatives; Britain's Economic Woes Split Tory Party, By Leonard Downie Jr., *Washington Post Foreign Service*, First Section; A1

the country had experienced minimal negative ramifications of Thatcher's laissez-faire, neo-liberal economic policies, in comparison with the North, such an upturn may well have not had the same impact as more deprived Northern areas of the country. Indeed, the average unemployment rate in the South during the period 1980-1984 was 7.1%, whilst in the North of the country 10.8% were out of work.[291] The implications of the results of the Mitcham and Morden by-election can be interpreted variably and from a range of perspectives due to the impossibility of determining the precise consequences of the contest. Having already considered the contextual perspective of events surrounding the Mitcham and Morden by-election, this chapter will now investigate the significance that the contest had in a wider context over the following years.

The most immediate deduction that can be made from the by-election was that it generally reflected public opinion towards the three main parties at the time, which was demonstrated a year later at the 1983 general election. Douglas-Mann's experience as an SDP candidate at Mitcham and Morden was felt nationwide more so by other members of the SDP arm of the Alliance, than the Liberal side. Indeed, the only SDP candidate to gain a seat at the 1983 election was Charles Kennedy.[292]

---

[291] D. Smith, *North and South: Britain's Economic Social and Political Divide* (London, 1994) p. 246
[292] R. Douglas, *Liberals: The history of the Liberals and Liberal Democrat Parties* (London, 2005) p.292

Furthermore, of the original 'Gang of Four' who formed the party, David Owen and Roy Jenkins were returned whilst Shirley Williams and Bill Rodgers were defeated.[293] Henceforth, as was witnessed at the Mitcham and Morden and the geographically distant Glasgow Hillhead elections which took place just a few months before, at a national level the Alliance with substantial, yet disparate support struggled to concentrate resources during the General Election campaign. Thus, with an impressive 25.4% of the national vote gained by the Alliance, reflected in a meagre 3.5% share of the seats in the 1983 election, the Alliance failed to recognise the importance in the concentration on specific seats, due to the disproportionality of the electoral system.[294] It is also interesting to note that in a joint statement by David Steel and Roy Jenkins in April 1983 "the Alliance parties had more than 500 candidates in the field," thereby seeing the weight of candidates as a positive rather than a negative for their electoral chances.[295] The lessons of playing to the strengths of the electoral system were not learnt however, which was evident at the following General Election. With such disparity apparent between the votes to seats at the 1983 election, the political lesson was not learnt by the time of the 1987 General Election where again, the Alliance gained a

---

[293] R. Douglas, *Liberals: The history of the Liberals and Liberal Democrat Parties* (London, 2005) p.292
[294] F.W.S. Craig, *British Electoral Facts, 1832-1987* (Aldershot, 1968) p.257
[295] *Ibid.*

significantly disproportionate number of seats to votes with 22.6% of the vote, yet only 3.4% of constituencies.[296]

The significance of the Mitcham and Morden result for the Conservatives can be interpreted in a variety of ways but the most obvious connotation is its indication of the unusual occurrence of public support for an incumbent government that would remain at a similar level up until the 1987 General Election. The result was also argued in a *Times* article on June 5th 1982, that "the lesson of the by-election is that Labour had become the more inviting target for the Alliance."[297] It must be taken into consideration additionally that the Liberal Party as well as the SDP were able to take seats from the Conservatives, with the Brecon and Radnor by-election as one such example of a Liberal gain from the Conservatives later in the parliament.[298] However, targeting by the SDP did not really develop and consequently the party concentrated their efforts evenly against both Labour and the Tories. In some localities this was met with success like at Portsmouth South in 1984 however, more often than not, the Alliance failed to capitalise on the national antipathy felt towards the Labour Party.[299] This can be reinforced with the fact that the last electoral gain made by the Alliance was done so at the expense

---

[296] *The Times*, 14th April 1983
[297] *The Times*, 5th June 1982
[298] *The Telegraph*, 26th September 2010
[299] 1984 Portsmouth South by-election results taken from www.parliament.co.uk/biographies accessed on Monday 18th March 2013

of Labour at Greenwich in February 1987.[300] Public opinion towards the Conservatives after the Mitcham and Morden by-election initially looked to be waning, with a defeat at the previously held Birmingham Northfield constituency in October 1982.[301] However, the 1983 General Election confirmed the continued lack of support for Labour, whilst the ability of the Conservatives to concentrate resources in specific seats led them to outflank the Alliance in converting votes into seats.

In diagnosing the significance of the Mitcham and Morden by-election, I believe that the result of the election played a greater significance both at a local and national level in the context the election was fought in at the time, as opposed to acting as an indicator of any future political developments. National issues such as the state of the economy, the Falklands conflict and the SDP split from the Labour Party, all in varying degrees contributed to Angela Rumbold's election. Of these, arguably the Falklands War was one of the least significant as the Conservatives would still have come out victorious due to their lead in opinion polls, alongside the fact that the widespread patriotic fervour did not affect the outcome of the Birmingham Northfield contest just months later. Moreover, after the election it is problematic to identify any patterns or themes in subsequent by-elections in the

---

[300] 1987 Greenwich by-election results taken from http://www.greenwichconservatives.com/election-results/greenwich-election-1987 accessed on 18th March 2013
[301] 1982 Birmingham Northfield by-election results taken from www.by-elections.co.uk/birmingham82.html accessed on 18th March 2013

following years that can be taken from this result, although the contest is useful in reflecting the popularity of the three main parties that was to be witnessed at the 1983 General Election.

Although local issues might not be considered as part of a wider context, Rumbold's appeal as a local candidate in a united party, in contrast to Douglas-Mann's more vulnerable position as a divisive figure in a fractured party, only further played into Rumbold's hands. Thus, an amalgamation of predominantly national factors, alongside less influential local issues played a role in causing the Mitcham and Morten by-election to be significant in accurately reflecting public opinion towards the three main political parties of the time, yet it cannot be seen as significant in gauging their longer term future popularity. The Conservative victory had the backdrop of the Falklands War but the SDP case for redefining the centre-left was overshadowed by the roar of the guns from the South Atlantic: not the case for Mrs Thatcher's government.

NORTHERN IRELAND: 1986
IAIN MILLER

On the 15th of November 1985 the Anglo-Irish Agreement was signed by Margret Thatcher and Garret FitzGerald, the then Taoiseach of Ireland, at Hillsborough Castle. The agreement gave greater powers to the Irish Government in Northern Irish governance whilst firmly asserting that the constitutional position of Northern Ireland would not change. For Unionists, believing in the continuation of Northern Irish separation from Ireland and the maintenance of the Northern Irish position within Britain, the agreement was a major political blow. It essentially ushered in an era of politics for Northern Ireland described as 'direct rule with a green tinge.'[302] In protest, all fifteen sitting Unionists Members of Parliament resigned their seats hoping that the ensuing by-

---

[302] H. Patterson, *Ireland Since 1939: The Persistence of Conflict*, (London, 2007) p.324

elections, held on 23rd January 1986, would prove the rejection of the agreement by the people of Northern Ireland.

This particularly turbulent political backdrop could lead to the assumption that the by-elections of 1986 were both significant and influential however, this is highly debateable. In order to fully address their significance they must firstly be treated as a whole set, in terms of what they are able to show and what they were able to achieve politically. Secondly some of the more important specific by-elections must be evaluated, in terms of their individual significance on a local level and to the by-elections as a whole. In order to assess the significance secondary sources have been used alongside primary sources, primarily in the form of newspaper articles from the period.

By 14th January 1986 campaigning for the Northern Ireland by-elections was well underway. Unionist candidates were keen to frame the numerous by-elections as being a referendum on the Anglo-Irish Agreement and, in voting for them, provided a chance for the people to vote in opposition to the controversial legislation. The campaign slogan 'Ulster says No!' was chosen to show this explicitly. The papers of the time however, were denouncing its significance before the by-elections had even occurred. *The Financial Times*, on the 14th of January, argued that actually the by-elections in January were simply 'testing the waters' for the Northern Ireland Assembly poll being held in October later that year.[303] The poll notably did not actually take place after the assembly was dissolved on 23rd June 1986 much to the displeasure of Unionist politicians. The newspaper, however, was obviously not to know this, and so arguing that the later election would ask the more pressing question of how far Unionist supporters are willing to share power with the Nationalists they delegitimised the January elections. [304] In labelling the by-elections as a 'howl of protest' the media created the image of noise without action, something used to impress with little substance.[305] This way of thinking labels the by-elections as a final show of strength from a party and a region that has already accepted that their political actions may not actually bear much significance to the wider Union. If *The Financial Times'* interpretation was sceptical of the significance of the by-elections then other sources from the time were wholly critical. *The Economist* observed that,

> 'Two months will then have passed since the two prime ministers signed their agreement. Parliamentary schedules, and the Christmas holidays, have already taken the lightning out of this substitute for the referendum the Unionists want.'[306]

---

[303] *The Financial Times*, 14th January 1986
[304] *Ibid.*
[305] *Ibid.*
[306] *The Economist* 4th January 1986

It therefore becomes apparent that opinion of the time saw these by-elections, even before they were counted, as a weak form of protest. In essence viewing the by-elections as a 'constitutional protest' against the Anglo-Irish Agreement means they lose significance. [307] By directing their protest at policy that had already been established the Unionists were speaking out at a force that, inevitably, they were unable to stop. As one paper describes at the time, 'The agreement is…an attitude of mind…it is not a building to be burned down or a set of laws to be repealed.'[308] Through this, no matter what the result of the by-elections, the extent to which this form of protest would be significant is being called into question.

Whilst the media predicted and debated over the by-elections before they had occurred there would, inevitably, be only one way to truly assess its significance, on the results. Voting took place on the 23rd January as, much to the Unionists despair, there were reports of 'bitterly cold winds, rain and sleet which lashed the province'.[309] The conditions however, were not a factor as the turnout increased since the last election. The votes spoke for themselves, Unionists polled 418,230 votes whilst the Alliance party managed only 32,095 'as Protestants voted for anti-

---

[307] J. Bardon, *A History of Ulster: New Updated Edition*, (Belfast, 2001) p.761
[308] *The Guardian*, 25th January 1986
[309] *The Financial Times*, 24th January 1986

agreement parties.'[310] The voting clearly showed that Ulster's Unionists had well and truly 'said no', but was this significant on a wider political level, or was it simply the swan song of a group that had lost their political power?

In order to assess the significance of the by-elections the degree of success for the Unionist party must be measured as, if the elections can't be seen as wholly successful, the Unionists would inevitably fail in their protest. Many sources from the time point to three significant areas that essentially reduced the impact of the by-elections for the Unionists. Firstly the original 'magic half a million'[311] votes desired by Unionists fell short by 81,770 votes. Without this total the Unionist vote did not drastically change from the previous election in 1983 and, consequently, it is difficult to argue whether the voting was clearly an anti-agreement vote or simply the continuation of Unionist political support. If the latter is true then the significance of the by-elections as a form of protest is drastically reduced. The second point highlighted was the 'upset caused by Mr Seamus Mallon, deputy leader of the SDLP' as he managed to take Newry and Armagh from the Unionist party.[312] This loss, looked into in more depth later, reduced the fifteen resigning Unionist MPs to fourteen, a notable loss for the Unionists, and therefore can be seen to further reduce the significance of the by-elections as an effective protest. Lastly,

---

[310] T. Hennessey, *A History of Northern Ireland 1920-1996*, (New York, 1997) p.274
[311] *The Observer*, 26th January 1986
[312] *The Financial Times*, 25th January 1986

highlighted by most sources from the time, was the 'drop for Sinn Fein and the IRA and an increase for the constitutional [Nationalist] party'.[313] Again, these figures are used to firstly suggest that there was pro-agreement feeling within Northern Ireland and that, as one paper writes 'the deal is already beginning to work.'[314] This once again reduces the significance of the by-elections as a form of protest.

Contemporary sources highlighting these three key areas all suggest that these elections were a failure for the Unionist parties that had to further their support within Northern Ireland, not just maintain it, in order to create a successful campaign. On top of this they suggest that as a series of elections designed to show a protest vote they lack political power against an agreement that is both difficult to directly attack but has powerful political support. There is however, a strong argument that, although the by-elections were not a sweeping success, they were significant in several ways.

Firstly, viewing the by-elections on a wider scale they can be seen as a pivotal moment in 'The Troubles' of Northern Ireland. A period characterised by violence as a form of protest, this is potentially one of the most significant political and non-violent displays of dissent towards the central policy of Westminster. In taking the bold move of mass resignation the fourteen returning

---

[313] *The Guardian*, 25th January 1986
[314] *The Observer*, 26th January 1986

Unionist MPs were armed with, what *The Guardian* described as, 'a fresh and convincing mandate', making the continuation of non-violent pressure a possibility.[315] When viewing the by-elections in this way the physical results become irrelevant as measuring success paves the way to simply seeing the fact that the by-elections occurred as significant. In showing 'a turn in Northern Irish society towards political solutions and away from violence as a viable option' the by-elections must be seen to be significant in furthering peaceful forms of protest.[316] This is not to say they put an end to violent reactions but that they were a progressive step towards that end.

The by-elections in 1986 also have significance when seen as part of a wider Unionist protest campaign. Sources from the time describe the Unionist alliance looking 'a little ragged', beginning to show 'cracks' and as stated before denounced the effectiveness of the by-elections as a form of protest.[317][318] However, if looking at the Unionists continual joint effort of resisting the Anglo-Irish Agreement through mass protests, council boycotts and lawsuits against the legality of the agreement, the by-elections are a significant factor in a wider political protest. They were the kick start to a 'huge demonstration of protest' from the

---

[315] *The Guardian*, 25th January 1986
[316] R. R. Rankin, 'Exorcising the Ghosts of Conflict in Northern Ireland: Stewart Parker's the Iceberg and Pentecost', *Eire-Ireland, 31, 3-4*, p.50
[317] *The Guardian*, 25th January 1986
[318] *The Observer*, 26th January 1986

Unionists.[319] It therefore becomes apparent that viewing these by-elections as a single significant event is not applicable, as is the case with other by-elections. Instead it must be seen as significant for being the beginning of a continual struggle, by all of the Unionist parties, against policy from Westminster.

Lastly the by-elections have significance when assessing them in terms of Northern Irish politics further down the line. The dissolving of the Northern Irish Assembly at Stormont in June 1986, mainly due to a lack of support from Nationalist politicians, meant that the by-elections of 1986 were the last major political elections held for the assembly. The official dissolution order states that dissolving the assembly occurred due to it being 'unlikely…that widely acceptable devolution proposals will be put forward' and 'that…[it is] in the public interest to dissolve it.'[320] This was again a negative impact for the Unionists who used the assembly to continue their protest against the Anglo-Irish Agreement and, with its closure, marked another failure to establish devolved government in Northern Ireland.

It is also necessary to address specific by-elections within the whole campaign, as particular by-elections held greater significance than others. Ian Paisley's campaign in North Antrim is often held up as holding particular significance to the by-elections

---

[319] P. Bew, *Ireland: The Politics of Enmity 1789-2006* (Oxford, 2007) pp.531-532
[320] Lord C. Lyell, 'Northern Ireland Assembly (Dissolution) Order 1986', *House of Lords Debate*, vol. 476, June 1986, p.1121

as a whole and specifically for the Democratic Unionist Party. Firstly, Paisley won 97.4% of the vote, the largest percentage polled by a candidate in a by-election for forty five years and, along with three other constituencies, was part of a group that were the last uncontested by other parties in British political history. Records aside the by-election can only hold significance if it is accepted that the Unionist protest was a success. Newspapers described this victory as the 'show of solidarity [drawing voters] behind the slogan 'Ulster Says No'' often pointing it out as the flagship for the Unionist cause, that truly showed the level of protest amongst the Northern Irish public. [321] There is however, the argument that, behind the records and overwhelming success, the by-elections actually symbolised the little significance the by-elections had as a protest. The Minister of State for Northern Ireland summed the government's ambivalence to the by-election results stating,

> 'the Government took the unionist vote seriously, but stressed that the agreement would be implemented.'[322]

Essentially the Paisley by-election in North Antrim, as stated before, symbolises the Unionist cause that, although they achieved a large majority representing protest votes against the

---

[321] *The Observer*, 26th January 1986
[322] *The Financial Times,* 25th January 1986

Anglo-Irish Agreement, it was essentially inconsequential. With Westminster's hard lined stance on the agreement, no matter the outcome it would have been implemented anyway which, in turn, delegitimises and reduces the significance of this specific by-election, and the by-elections as a whole as an effective form of protest and sign of dissent.

The other by-election that held particular significance in 1986 was the Newry and Armagh contest. The marginal victory went to the SDLP candidate Seamus Mallon, primarily seen as representing the pro-agreement stance. This victory for the pro-agreement SDLP was highlighted by many at the time as significant defeat for the Unionists. *The New York Times* significantly addressed the specific by-election at the top of its article which essentially described the result in Newry and Armagh as the main reason to question whether 'Ulster said no…loudly enough?'[323] Other newspapers followed a similar trend of pointing out the SDLP win early on in their articles.[324][325] If North Antrim is seen as the Unionists flagship by-election, proving anti-agreement sentiment amongst the Unionist public, then Newry and Armagh is equally important to the SDLP and Nationalists that took a pro-agreement stance. It is also pointed out by one newspaper that the SDLP victory in Newry and Armagh gave them,

---

[323] *The New York Time*, 26th January 1986
[324] *The Financial Times,* 25th January 1986
[325] *The Observer*, 26th January 1986

'*more* direct input [in devolution talks] – ironically, than the Unionist majority since the Unionist leaders started to boycott the Northern Ireland Office.'[326]

In electing this one new MP the SDLP were able to successfully oppose the Unionists, if only in one seat, in getting their fifteen MPs re-elected, meaning the by-elections were never able to be called a resounding success. As addressed before, the general opinion was that the Unionists had achieved a large majority but this result, in a single by-election, significantly allowed Westminster, Nationalists, and any other pro-agreement groups to show failings in the Unionist 'referendum' on the Anglo-Irish Agreement.

When assessing the significance of the by-elections in Northern Ireland in 1986 it is important to see them as both individual by-elections and as a whole. Far too often generalised as a single block election the by-elections individually represented different things in different counties.

This being said, the fifteen Unionist candidates seeking re-election and a renewed mandate saw these by-elections as a referendum and, unlike many other by-elections in UK political history, these were portrayed by the media to have one sole focus: the Anglo-Irish agreement. This controversial issue, therefore, is

---

[326] *The Guardian*, 25th January 1986

the main measurement of significance and how far we can view these by-elections as influential. Essentially when viewing the by-elections as a group their aim was to put pressure on the UK government to change the agreement, an aim in which they failed. It is therefore a convincing argument to state that these by-elections actually held little significance as a form of protest and put little political pressure on a government that denounced their significance from their outset.

Assessing the significance of these by-elections solely on their political impact is however, rather short sighted. Firstly, these by-elections were a non-violent display of political opinion. A process that, although it did not signal the end to 'The Troubles' in Northern Ireland, did show a progressive step to increasingly peaceful displays of protest, something that is significant in Northern Ireland's history. Secondly, although when observed as a single event these by-elections were not particularly successful, they must be viewed as part of the continuing Unionist struggle. When seen as the starting point and the affirming of popular support for Unionist pressure on Westminster their influence becomes more significant. These by-elections did not create much change however, the ongoing Unionist campaign did. Perhaps more sentimentally, these were the last official electoral events conducted by Northern Irish politicians under the Stormont Assembly before its dissolution in June later that year. Just as with the point that this was the largest collection of by-elections on one single day in UK political history; this point may not have particular political influence but symbolically is still significant. Finally, the specific by-elections in North Antrim and Newry and Armagh hold particular significance amongst the other by-elections as they are often held up as the significant victories for both sides of the dispute between the Anglo-Irish Agreement.

It therefore becomes apparent that, if viewing these by-elections' significance solely on their independent success then it is difficult to argue that they held any significance at all. Their primary aim of preventing the Anglo-Irish Agreement was not fulfilled, their total votes compared the previous 1983 election did not significantly increase and they did not return all fifteen sitting Unionist MPs.

However, as address before, this is a short-sighted perception of what happened in 1986. When viewing these by-elections as non-violent forms of protest and as a continuation of the wider unified Unionist campaign against Westminster it is undeniable that they hold significance, not only in Northern Irish, but in the UK's political history.

As Ian Paisley, James Molyneaux and Enoch Powell continued their political pressure beyond 1986; these by-elections could always be recalled, not as a resounding success, but as a significant point for Unionist peaceful and influential protest against Westminster government. Deciding governance in Northern Ireland bilaterally with the Dublin, without recourse to the population of Northern Ireland through a referendum was not acceptable to Unionists: a principle that would be vital in the eventual resolution on 'The Troubles' by successor governments.

DUNFERMLINE AND WEST FIFE: 2006
WILLIE RENNIE

The Dunfermline and West Fife by-election in February 2006 should have been a straightforward success for the Labour Party. It is a traditional Labour seat which is so deeply Labour that part of the constituency was once represented by Willie Watson and future Prime Minister, Gordon Brown.. The victory for the Liberal Democrats was secured despite the party facing a number of problems which should have resulted in a falling, not rising vote. With the Scottish National Party only one year away from victory in the Scottish Parliament Elections in 2007 a challenge from that party should have been more likely.

The campaign was conducted in freezing conditions over a truncated three week period following the premature passing of the previous Member Rachel Squire who had held the seat since 1992.

She had built up a substantial majority securing half the total votes cast in the election held the previous year when the Prime Minister, Tony Blair, won a slender majority in Parliament on a smaller share of the vote. In Dunfermline the Liberal Democrats had a marginally higher share of the vote than the Scottish National Party on 20% each and the Conservatives secured less than a tenth of the vote.

The politics of the area had been dominated by the Labour Party. They ran Fife Council with fifteen councillors locally. The Liberal Democrats had five local councillors in the central and southern parts of Dunfermline. The Scottish National Party had one council seat and two independents represented the far west of Fife and the north of the town. The first past the post system had delivered dominance by the Labour Party who had, as a result, run the council for decades. This had generated weariness amongst the voters who felt that the party had taken them for granted with little effort required for re-election.

Dunfermline had gone through significant transformation in the years prior to 2006 with a considerable expansion in new housing accommodating commuters for Edinburgh. Other significant employers included defence with traditional employers at Rosyth Dockyard and more recent employers BAE Systems and Rolls Royce at Dalgety Bay. Other sectors included: the oil industry servicing the North Sea; financial sector with the Bank of Scotland and Dunfermline Building Society; a major call centre with Sky and energy generation at Longannet Power Station. Other than the latter and a sprinkling of opencast mines with small numbers of employees the long standing relationship with coal had come to an end. The traditional unionised and state dependent sectors were being gradually edged out by new industries and sectors with more middle class employees. The Labour Party's ability to influence these new sectors was now more limited and put other parties on a more equal footing.

Despite the dramatic expansion of homes, and therefore population, in West Fife the area's local hospital, Queen Margaret, had been the subject of a decision by the Health Board to downgrade it and move Accident and Emergency and specialist healthcare to Kirkcaldy. The local community had campaigned strongly against the decision over a long period. The local protest was both about civic pride, for the town that regards itself as a city, and local healthcare needs but resentment of the Labour establishment was considerable. The campaign had put up a candidate at the 2003 Scottish Parliamentary Election winning 18% of the vote and at the concurrent council elections secured the election of a councillor in the hospital ward. Even though the decision to downgrade the hospital had been confirmed by the Labour led Scottish Executive several years before there was still much disquiet locally which was primarily targeted at the Labour Party.

The growing population of Edinburgh of how commuters were to be transported into the capital by road and rail made the road link over the Forth Estuary the subject of much debate. Firstly, the forty year old road bridge had been found to be losing strength with increasing alarm that it may be closed to heavy goods vehicles within years. Secondly, to contribute towards tackling climate change, limit car volumes in the city and pay for the maintenance of the crossing the Forth Estuary Transport Authority was about to agree to increase the £1 toll to £4. There was a lot of opposition to the toll increase which was seen to be unfair to Fife commuters as no other community around Edinburgh was subject to a charge to enter the city. The Labour Party dominated FETA so faced most of the anger. The suggested replacement of the bridge with a new crossing was controversial with some environmental groups and business bodies but failed to penetrate the wider electorate.

The final key issue for local voters was the state of Dunfermline's city centre which was dominated by the shell of the old and once grand Co-op building at the bottom and tired end of the High Street. This symbolised the failure of a once fine shopping centre that was now failing to attract the considerable new population in the east of the city. The Labour establishment once again were blamed for this failure.

Labour's dominance was also signified by neighbouring Member of Parliament. The soon to be Prime Minister, and then

Chancellor, Gordon Brown lived in the constituency and represented the neighbouring constituency of Kirkcaldy and Cowdenbeath. He once represented, prior to the then recent boundary changes, a large part of the Dunfermline and West Fife constituency so there was a lot of affection and association with Gordon Brown.

So far I have set out the changing conditions in the constituency and the dominant issues. I will now describe the campaign.

The Labour Party had chosen MEP, and Dunfermline based, Catherine Stihler to fight the seat after a controversial selection process with allegations of headquarters intervention. Our campaign sought to exploit that dissent highlighting that she did not give up her seat in the European Parliament which implied that Labour were not confident she would win and led to criticism that she was seeking two jobs. The Conservatives had similar difficulties with a Fife Councillor over looked in favour of an articulate female candidate from another part of the region. The Scottish National Party chose local man Douglas Chapman with me chosen as the Liberal Democrat candidate. As a Fifer I had strong local credentials which the campaign made much of. My grandfather was a local minister, my father the grocer and I was runner up in the Scottish Coal Carrying Championship held locally. The campaign portrayed me as the Liberal Democrats version of the Scottish cartoon character 'Oor Willie' with a specially produced cartoon featuring me sat on a bucket. The Editor of *The Sunday Post* – the home of Oor Wullie – was not best pleased.

Catherine Stihler was several months pregnant during the campaign which none of the party campaigns sought to use to their advantage but was an issue that was raised with canvassers on the doorstep. Some letters were published in the local newspaper, *The Dunfermline Press*. It created some discomfort for me, and I am sure the other candidates, as this was irrelevant to Catherine Stihler's suitability or otherwise to represent the area.

The initial phase of the campaign was establishing who had the best chance of challenging the Labour Party's grip on the constituency. The southern end settlements of Inverkeithing and Rosyth were identified as important areas for targeting with messages to persuade nationalist supporters that their party of preference had little chance of success and that only the Liberal Democrats could win. Those communities had relatively high levels of support for the SNP.

However, the campaign for the Liberal Democrats was dogged by numerous scandals and errors that many thought would engulf the effort and destine the party to a plummeting share of the vote. Charles Kennedy had recently resigned as Party Leader over his relationship with alcohol and concern from colleagues that he was unable to do his job effectively. He was seen to have been forced out unreasonably which created resentment amongst party members and supporters especially in his heartland of Scotland. During the election campaign two of the leadership contenders to replace Charles Kennedy were engulfed in sex related scandals. A minute of a meeting of Liberal Democrat MPs was leaked revealing that they thought the Party's chances of victory were limited and that it would do well to hold second place. Other, more minor, mistakes created the impression of chaos.

However, this chaos mattered little as voters focussed on what mattered to them. I recall reading the latest set of dreadful headlines in the Sunday newspapers considering whether the campaign was worth the effort. Instead of festering and imagining the reaction of the voters we decided to test it for ourselves. Either the voters had not read the papers or thought it irrelevant but whichever it was the response was uplifting. Only two households mentioned the scandals – one I subsequently discovered was not an admirer of any politician and the other laughed with us about our difficulties and confirmed they would continue to support us. As our campaign continued to grow, through the three week election, this momentum countered any suggestion that the party was wholly dysfunctional and incapable of victory. This is an important lesson for candidates in elections where their campaigns are immersed in problems. Sometimes the issues that the national media think critical are irrelevant to the priorities of the voters.

Gordon Brown directed much of the campaign and appeared frequently with the candidate throughout the election. He made a number of direct media interventions with bold commitments and promises which perhaps may have been seen as unrealistic and purely concocted for the election campaign. He first promised that a new crossing over the Forth would be built to replace the Forth Road Bridge. Then he made a commitment to bring an international business school to the city. Both issues, whilst important, were not seen to be central to the concerns of local people which reinforced the failure of the Labour Party to remain connected with a traditional Labour constituency. Gordon Brown was seen to have a focus more in London than in Fife which, whilst not unreasonable, compounded the problems that the Labour Party was facing locally.

Our campaign privately mocked the future Prime Minister for his sudden and dramatic promises. One supporter said G Brown would build the new bridge in not years, nor months but days or maybe even hours with a new miracle metal made out of every day substances such as coke cans and thin air.

This was the first by-election campaign for David Cameron since he became Conservative Party Leader only months before. Without high expectations it was seen as the first test of his new strategy of reaching out to new voters. He attempted to woo Liberal Democrat supporters by claiming that his new strategy meant that the Liberal Democrats were the same as the

Conservatives so Liberal Democrat supporters should switch to Conservative. The Liberal Democrat campaign used this to persuade Conservative supporters to do the opposite. Many did.

Alex Salmond had returned to the Leadership of the Scottish National Party after a four year interruption when the Party, under the Leadership of John Swinney, had seen a slump in support at several elections. The Party had only recently failed to win the Livingston By-election after the death of Robin Cook so was hungry for a win over the other side of the Forth estuary. Yet the SNP campaign lacked penetration. It failed to connect with voters on the issues they considered important.

The Liberal Democrat campaign outgunned the others with both the quality and quantity of literature and the extent of the door and telephone canvassing. I led afternoon and evening canvassing sessions seven days a week for the bulk of the campaign and when not doing interviews or debates visited almost every shop and business in the constituency. The micro campaigning focussed on personal and local issues seeking to resolve problems with issues as diverse as parks to personal finance. The team of four caseworkers were fed with my daily returns scribbled on scraps of paper often soaking wet from the winter rain. Farmers were recruited to display posters in their fields and even young supporters were sent with super posters to stand at roundabouts and on the access to the Forth Road Bridge on polling day.

The mantra of a 'Fifer fighting for Fife' for the hospital, against the tolls rise and for the High Street contrasted well with the Labour Party who seemed tired and out of touch.

Despite this the pollsters and commentators predicted that the contest would be a close race between the SNP and Labour which led the local newspaper, *The Dunfermline Press*, to report "It's close" one week before polling day. This was based on the judgement of Professor John Curtice who is regarded as the foremost psephologist in Scottish, and arguably UK, politics. Because of the internal problems within the Liberal Democrats few thought it likely that victory was even possible.

It was only during the last weekend of the campaign that it become clear across the parties that the Liberal Democrats were gaining momentum and could win.

The BBC, probably advised by John Curtice himself, decided not to hold an election night programme to cover the count but when it became clear that my victory was likely the BBC hastily cobbled together experts to speak on the result. John Curtice was one of those experts.

The weekly, then daily leaflet deliveries; the massive and growing poster campaign; the hours of candidate canvassing (rain, hail, snow, shine or freezing rain); the daily media visits with party VIPs; the big canvassing teams on the doors and on the phones built the momentum.

Our frequent but brief walkabouts or parades in the town centre were impressive with large numbers of supporters with Lib Dem diamonds handing out stickers and inviting voters to meet me. It was a show of strength and compared well with the lonely Labour efforts.

But perhaps it was the return of Charles Kennedy that signalled victory was near. His short, but significant, visit to Dunfermline High Street attracted the nation's media to report that he was back and was warmly received by the people of Dunfermline. "We love you Charles" was the call from one supporter that captured the atmosphere of the day. The media scrum that day was a potentially dangerous affair but frequent shouts of "bollard" warned the moving mass to beware of the protruding street furniture below.

Whilst the other campaigns flagged as we neared the finish line our campaign grew in confidence.

The day before polling day Nicol Stephen ventured, with permission, to the top of the iconic Forth Bridge. It was a stunning, sunny day with hardly a cloud in the sky. The pooled photographer snapped a confident leader and candidate on top of the world apparently ready to win. We featured in many newspapers including the front of the regional *Courier*. The exposure on all the newsstands gave us the final lift we needed.

The indications of growing support were also anecdotal. People stopping their cars in the middle of busy main streets to shout support at the top of their voices. Others advising that I was the man they were all talking about. And meeting a rather downbeat Alex Salmond in a café in Kincardine Bridge on polling day, clearly resigned to defeat.

Analysing postal ballots revealed that there was momentum with the Liberal Democrats. The first count of the earliest voters had both the Liberal Democrats and Labour evenly matched. The second, admittedly more limited, count gave the Liberal Democrats a significant lead.

The final result gave the Liberal Democrats a 1,800 majority, and a 13% swing, over Labour. It was the first time Labour had lost a seat at a Westminster by-election in Scotland since the Scottish National Party won the Glasgow Govan by-election in 1988, and the first time Labour has ever lost to the Liberal Democrats, or their predecessors the Liberal Party, in a Scottish Westminster by-election.

That it was lost with the Liberal Democrats in power in the Scottish Parliament in the midst of personal scandals made the loss even more bitter for the Labour Party. It is unusual for parties to gain by-elections when in power especially when they are reaching the end of their time in power. To win with such a large shift in the vote is rare. There had not been such a victory in thirty years of by-election history.

The ramifications of the result were extensive.

It gave the Liberal Democrats an escape from the party's problems. The internal difficulties were clearly of little consequence to voters who were more alert to the issues at the heart of the local community. This enabled the party to recover from the multitude of crises that had engulfed the party and calmed the fears of activists about the significance of the difficulties.

For Labour the ramifications were even more significant. To lose in Gordon Brown's home territory was a blow to the apparent invincibility of the Chancellor who was actively working to replace the then Prime Minister Tony Blair. But it affected the Prime Minister too. He had lost a safe seat within months of a third General Election victory. For the Labour led Scottish Executive, uncomfortably in partnership with the Liberal Democrats, it reinforced the impression that it had run out of steam. For Labour run Fife Council is signalled that they could no longer take the area for granted.

With the Scottish National Party the result showed that despite its claims of being the challenger to the Labour Party in Scotland it had taken another party to topple Labour for the first time in almost twenty years. The newly re-elected leader, Alex

Salmond, had failed to recover the SNPs fortunes despite much "bluff and bluster."

David Cameron didn't expect to make advances and his expectations were met.

The longer term effects of the by-election were more limited. It contributed to future trends but did not create those trends by itself. Gordon Brown's unsure handling of the Labour campaign was later replicated in his subsequent premiership. Perhaps it led to the subsequent loss of power by Labour in the Scottish Parliament with the SNP eventually securing one more seat than Labour in the elections which took place in 2007.

For the Liberal Democrats it gave evidence that victory was possible in adversity but did not signal a significant rise in support nationwide, nor did it deliver additional seats in the Scottish Parliament – in fact the party lost one seat in the elections a year later. The party did, however, gain the Scottish Parliamentary seat of Dunfermline West and an increase of three seats on Fife Council.

Allegations of "Weapons of Mass Deception" were directed at the Liberal Democrat campaign over the issue of tolls where it was said that the Liberal Democrats claimed to oppose their increase when it was Liberal Democrat councillors voted for the proposal. This was discounted by the Liberal Democrats who identified that the vote did not adhere to party affiliation. But how much they understand workings of FETA is doubtful.

It is traditional for famous by-election wins to result in an immediate loss at the subsequent General Election. The Party instituted a four year campaign to retain the seat which included winning support through providing support, advice and advocacy services to constituents. This was complemented by year round communications campaign of newsletters, canvassing and new media. Annual community and business tours in addition to weekly press operation meant that I was highly visible and active.

The issues evolved with the tolls, hospital and High Street gradually fading as issues to be replaced by more dominant concerns including the economy, jobs, the new aircraft carriers and the Rosyth dockyard, the future of Longannet Power Station and the replacement of the Forth Road Bridge.

The Labour Party managed to recover from defeat in 2006 and 2007 to choose a new candidate and invested people and finance to build a team to win.

The Liberal Democrat challenge of retaining the seat was still perceived as possible with the strength of the local campaign. With the rising popularity of leader Nick Clegg it was considered even more likely that a victory could be delivered.

Yet with a simple but effective message that only Labour or Conservatives could form the next Government and the Liberal Democrats were too close to the Conservatives. The anti-Thatcher campaign of the 1990s was resurrected to remind voters of the effect on the constituency the last time the Conservatives were in power.

I lost the election in 2010 by 5,000 votes.

I will always remember those three weeks in late winter with great warmth. It was a testing time for the party but revealed an inner strength and resilience which it would later find critical to enduring the coalition with the Conservatives. The victory was even sweeter because it was not expected and it was in an area we would never expect to win under normal circumstances.

After my first week at Westminster I recall driving back from the airport over the Forth Road Bridge on a sunny winter's day. I looked over to the grand Victorian rail bridge, up to the Longannet Power Station, far over to Knockhill racing track, the dockyard and Dunfermline Abbey in the centre. It was a wonderful scene that I had observed on many occasions before but this time was different.

BIBLIOGRAPHY

Books

S. Ball, *The Conservative Party and British Politics 1902-1951*, (Harlow, 1995)

J. Bardon, *A History of Ulster: New Updated Edition*, (Belfast, 2001)

P. Bew, *Ireland: The Politics of Enmity 1789-2006* (Oxford, 2007)

D. Butler and A. Sloman, *British Political Facts 1900-1979*, fifth edition (US, 1980)

D. Butler, 'By-elections and their interpretation' in *By-elections in British Politics*, (London, 2003)

E. A. Cameron, *Impaled Upon a Thistle: Scotland Since 1880,* (Edinburgh, 2010)

C. Cook, 'The Challengers to the Two-Party System' in *Trends in British Politics since 1945*, London, 1978)

F. W. S. Craig, *British Electoral Facts, 1832-1987* (Aldershot,

1968)

F. W. S. Craig, *British Parliamentary Election Results 1918-1949, 3rd Ed.* (Surrey, 1983)

G. Dawson, *Making Peace with the Past: Memory, Trauma and the Irish Troubles.* (Manchester, 2007)

R. Douglas, *Liberals: The history of the Liberals and Liberal Democrat Parties* (London, 2005)

D. Dutton, *A History of the Liberal Party in the Twentieth Century,* (Basingstoke, 2004)

R. English, *Irish freedom: the History of Nationalism in Ireland* (London, 2007)

D. G. Evans, *A History of Wales 1906-2000,* (Wales, 2000)

G. Evans, *Black Paper on Wales 1967,* (Cardiff, 1967)

G. Evans, *For the Sake of Wales,* Second Edition, (Wales, 1996)

G. Evans, *Welsh Nationalist Aims,* (Carmarthen, 1968)

M. Foot and A. Highet, *Isaac Foot: A Westcountry Boy - Apostle of England: A Plymouth Boy* (London, 2006)

A. Fort, *Nancy: The Story of Lady Astor*, (New York, 2012)

T. Hennessey, *A History of Northern Ireland 1920-1996*, (New York, 1997)

T. Hennessey, *Hunger Strike: Margaret Thatcher's Battle with the IRA.* (Kildare, 2014)

M. Hilson, *Political Change And the Rise of Labour in Comparative Perspective: Britain And Sweden, 1890-1930* (Lancaster, 2006)

I. G. C. Hutchison, *Scottish Politics in the Twentieth Century* (Basingstoke, 2001)

J. G. Jones, *A Radical Life: The Biography of Megan Lloyd George* (London, 1991)

P. Lynch, *SNP, The History of the Scottish National Party,* (Cardiff, 2002)

Sir A. M. MacEwen, *The Thistle and the Rose: Scotland's Problems To-day,* (Edinburgh, 1932)

L. McAllister, *Plaid Cymru: The Emergence of a Political Party,* (Bridgend, 2001)

I. McBride, *History and Memory in Modern Ireland* (Cambridge, 2001)

D. McKittrick, and D. McVeigh, *Making Sense of the Troubles.* (London, 2001)

L. Mowat, *Britain Between the Wars, 1918-1940* (London, 1968)

C. Moore *Margaret Thatcher: the Authorised Biography. Volume 1, Not for Turning.* (London, 2013)

B. O'Brien, 1999. *The Long War: The IRA and Sinn Fein* (New York, 1999)

R. O'Rawe, *Blanketmen* (Dublin, 2005)

A. Sandry, *Plaid Cymru: An Ideological Analysis,* (Wales, 2011)

B. Sands, *Writings from Prison.* (Lanham, 1997)

A. Seldon, and D. Collings, *Britain Under Thatcher* (London, 2000)

R. Self 'Fighting One's Own Friends is Hateful Work: Coalition troubles January – October 1922' in R. Self (ed.) *The Austen Chamberlain Diary Letters. The Correspondence of Sir Austen Chamberlain with his Sisters Hilda and Ida 1916-1937* (Camden, 1995) Fifth Series Vol. 5

D. Smith, *North and South: Britain's Economic Social and Political Divide* (London, 1994)

H. Stephenson, *Claret and Chips, The Rise of the SDP* (London, 1982)

J. Stevenson, *Third Party Politics since 1945, Liberals, Alliance and Liberal Democrats*, (London, 1993)

N. Stockley, *Dictionary of Liberal Biography*, (London, 1998)

P. Taylor, *Beyond the Mask: The IRA and Sinn Fein.* (New York, 1997)

M. Thatcher, *The Autobiography.* (London, 1995)

A. Thorpe, *A History of the British Labour Party, 3rd Ed.*, (London, 2008)

P. Ward, *Unionism in the United Kingdom 1918-1974*, (Basingstoke, 2005)

Statistical Sources

1801 - 1981 Census figures, Merton Council

1979- 1983 Polls, NOP/Daily Mail Poll 5th February 1982

1979- 1983 Polls, Gallup/Telegraph Poll 12th April 1982

1982 Birmingham Northfield by-election results

1984 Portsmouth South by-election results taken from

www.parliament.co.uk/biographies accessed on Monday 18th March 2013

1987 Greenwich by-election results taken from http://www.greenwichconservatives.com/election-results/greenwich-election-1987 accessed on 18th March 2013

CAIN, Chronology of the Conflict – 1981, 2013

The Falklands War - Panel Survey, Published June 1982, Fieldwork 14 April - 23 June 1982, IPSOS Mori

R. Kimber, *General Election Results October 1959*

R. Kimber, *General Election Results March 1966*

R. Kimber, *General Election Results October 1964*

Government Papers

Hansard, HC Deb 28 December 1919, vol 123, cols 250-2

Lord C. Lyell, 'Northern Ireland Assembly (Dissolution) Order 1986', *House of Lords Debate*, vol. 476, June 1986

Northern Ireland Executive. *Ministers and their Departments*, 2014

Representation of the People Act 1918, *UK Parliament*

Representation of the People Act 1981, *UK Parliament*

M. Thatcher, March 5th 1981 House of Commons Prime Minister's Questions

Interviews

Danny Morrison, interviewed by Rory Tinman. 2013

Richard O'Rawe, interviewed by Rory Tinman. 2014

Journal Articles

Anon. 'Before and After The British Election' *Advocate of Peace Through Justice 84* (1922)

J. Ault 'The Inter – War Cornish By- Elections: Microcosm of 'Rebellion'?' in P. Payton (ed.) *Cornish Studies 20* (Exeter, 2012)

D. Balsom 'Plaid Cymru: the Welsh National Party' in H.M. Drucker (ed.) *Multi-Party Britain* (Basingstoke, 1979)

D. Butler 'By-elections and their interpretation' in *By-elections in British Politics* (London, 2003)

M. Ceadel 'The First British Referendum: The Peace Ballot 1934-35' *The English Historical Review 95 377* (October 1980)

C. Cook 'The Challengers to the Two-Party System' *Trends in British Politics since 1945* (London, 1978)

J. O. Edwards 'The Early History of the Counties of Carmarthen and Cardigan' *The English Historical Review* (1916)

J. G. Jones 'A Breach in the Family' *The Journal of Liberal Democrat History* (1999)

I. McAllister '"The Armalite and the ballot box": Sinn Fein's electoral strategy in Northern Ireland.' In *Electoral Studies 23* (2004)

R. I. Mckibbin 'James Ramsay Macdonald and the Problem of the Independence of the Labour Party 1910-1914' *The Journal of*

Modern History 42 (June 1970)

D. Moen 'Irish Political Prisoners and Post Hunger-Strike Resistance to Criminalisation.' *British Society of Criminology.* Vol. 3. (1999)

K. Morgan 'David Lloyd George' in J. Mackintosh (ed.) *British Prime Ministers in the Twentieth Century: Balfour to Chamberlain* (London, 1977)

K. Morgan 'Lloyd George's Premiership: A Study in 'Prime Ministerial Government' *The Historical Journal 13* (March 1970)

A. Mughan 'On the By-Election Vote of Governments in Britain' *Legislative Studies Quarterly 13* (1988)

S. Price and D. Sanders 'By-Elections Changing Fortunes Uncertainty and the Mid-Term Blues' *Public Choice 95* (1998)

R. R. Rankin 'Exorcising the Ghosts of Conflict in Northern Ireland: Stewart Parker's the Iceberg and Pentecost' *Eire-Ireland 31 3-4* (1996)

G. L. Reid 'Plymouth to Parliament: A Rhetorical History of Nancy Astor's 1919 Campaign by Karen J. Musolf' *A Quarterly Journal Concerned with British Studies 32* (2000)

J. A. Thompson 'The Historians and the Decline of the Liberal Party' *Albion: A Quarterly Journal Concerned with British Studies 22* (Spring 1990) and D. Powell 'The New Liberalism and the Rise of Labour 1886-1906' *The Historical Journal 29* (June 1986)

I. Turok and N. Edge 'The jobs gap in Britain's cities: Employment loss and labour market consequences' *The Policy Press* (1999)

T. Wilson 'The Coupon and the British General Election of 1918' *The Journal of Modern History* 36 1 (1964)

News Outlets

Anderstown News

Associated Press

BBC News

Belfast Telegraph

The Daily Mail

The Economist

The Evening Times

The Financial Times

The Glasgow Herald

The Guardian

The Independent

Irish Central

The New York Times

The Observer

Pathé News

Saturday Review of Politics, Literature, Science and Art

The Scotsmen Today

The Star

The Telegraph

The Times

United Press International

Washington Post Foreign Service

Western Daily Mercury

Western Morning News

Speeches

M. Thatcher, *1981 March 5th speech in Belfast.*
http://www.margaretthatcher.org/document/104589.

Websites

Bobby Sands Trust 'Florence names Bobby Sands St.' *Bobby Sands Trust.* Available at: http://www.bobbysandstrust.com/archives/2570

G. Evans, *Wales Resurgent.* Available at: http://www.youtube.com/watch?v=_ms6JFJqpU0

W. W. Knox, 'A History of the Scottish People: Summary of Economy and Society in Scotland 1840-1940' *SCRAN.* Available at: http://www.scran.ac.uk/scotland/pdf/SP2_10Economy.pdf

D. Russell 'History Lessons For The Conservatives and Liberal Democrats.' *Click on Wales.* Available at: http://www.clickonwales.org/2012/10/history-lessons-for-the-conservatives-and-liberal-democrats/

INDEX

Adams, Gerry, 114

Asquith, Herbert H., 37, 42, 55

Astor, Nancy, 18-19, 21-30, 33-34

Benn, Tony, 9

Blair, Tony, 12, 80, 86, 148, 159

Blaney, Neil, 101

Bowen, John W., 36

Brown, Gordon, 11, 147, 150-154, 159-160

Cameron, David, 12, 154, 159

Campbell, Menzies, 12

Carrington, Peter, 121

Carron, Owen, 103, 105, 107, 110-113, 116-117

Chamberlain, Austen, 14, 39

Chapman, Douglas, 151

Chullin, Caral Ni, 114

Clarry, Reginald, 36

Devlin McAliskey, Bernadette, 97

Dilk, John, 81

Douglas-Mann, Bruce, 120-125, 127, 130

Evans, Gwynfor, 10, 15, 61-64, 68-69, 71-73

Ewing, Winnie, 10

FitzGerald, Garret, 17, 133

Foot, Isaac, 19, 22-23, 25, 28, 31, 33

Foster, Arlene, 117

Gaitskell, Hugh, 85

Galtieri, Leopoldo, 119

Gay, William T., 22, 27-28, 34

Gibney, Jim, 97

Guinness, Jonathan, 81

Haslam, Lewis, 36-37

Havers, Sir Michael, 106

Heath, Edward, 126

Hughes, Simon, 12

Hughes, Emry, 74

Huhne, Chris, 12

Jackson, Margaret, 88

Jenkins, Roy, 128

Kennedy, Charles, 12, 127, 152, 157

Lindsay, Kenneth M., 47

Livingston, Mackenzie, 50

Lloyd George, Megan, 14-15, 61-75

Lloyd George, David, 13-14, 22, 32, 39-42, 61, 64

Lubbock, Eric, 84

MacDonald, Ramsey, 48

MacEwen, Alexander, 11, 51-56

Maguire, Frank, 96

Maguire, Noel, 99

Mallon, Seamus, 17, 137, 142

Markiewicz, Constance, 24

McCartney, Raymond, 114

McGuiness, Martin, 114

Molyneaux, Jim, 145

Moore, Lyndon W., 36

Morrison, Danny, 95-102, 104-105, 109-113

Nicholas, David, 121-122

O'Rawe, Richard, 93, 97-98, 100, 103, 105, 107-109, 114-115

Owen, David, 128

Paisley, Ian, 17, 141-142, 145

Powell, Enoch, 145

Prior, Jim, 112

Rennie, Willie, 11

Rodgers, Bill, 128

Rumbold, Angela, 19, 119-124, 130-131

Salmond, Alex, 13, 155, 158, 159-160

Sands, Bobby, 15-16, 91-116

Sheehan, Pat, 114

Squire, Rachel, 147

Steel, David, 128

Stephen, Nicol, 157

Stihler, Catherine, 151-152

Taverne, Dick, 19-20, 79-90

Thatcher, Margaret, 15, 17, 19, 95-96, 98, 101, 106-126, 133, 161

West, Harry, 99-100, 104-105, 109

Williams, Shirley, 128

Wilson, Harold, 80, 85-86

Printed in Great Britain
by Amazon